HURRY!

Hurry

My

Children

HURRY!

Hurry

My

Children

Labertha Theresa Darensbourg-McCormick
Also known
As
"Mama Lulu"
"Illustrations by Labertha McCormick"
Cover Photograph by Lawrence Clark

Copyright © Labertha Theresa Darensbourg-McCormick.

All rights reserved. No part of this book may be reproduced in any form or by any electronic or mechanical means, including information storage and retrieval systems, without permission in writing from the publisher, except by reviewers, who may quote brief passages in a review.

ISBN: 978-1-64606-724-4 (Paperback Edition)
ISBN: 978-1-64606-725-1 (Hardcover Edition)
ISBN: 978-1-64606-723-7 (E-book Edition)

Some characters and events in this book are fictitious. Any similarity to real persons, living or dead, is coincidental and not intended by the author.

Scripture taken from the National American Bible (NAB).

Book Ordering Information

Phone Number: 347-901-4929 or 347-901-4920
Email: info@globalsummithouse.com
Global Summit House
www.globalsummithouse.com

Printed in the United States of America

Contents

Acknowledgements xiii
Little Old Lady 1
A Tribute To Rudy 3
Fore-Word 4
Memo Letter 9
Hurry, Hurry My Children 10
IF's 14
An excerpt letter 15
Listen To The Elders 16
Hurried Help 17
Grand Ma's Feet 18
Healing Powers 20
Speak Easy 21
Nappy Headed 24
Common Woman 26
You're Stuck 29
I am the Black Woman 31
What Should I Tell My Child Whose Head Is Long? 34
My Child 36
Lazy Boy 37
A Shuck Time Poet 38
No Time For Poetry 39
A Nice Party 40
Calling All Po' Folk 41
"I Ain't Got Nobody..." 42
The Lucky Ones 45

The Wind	46
Twinkle, Twinkle	47
—Walk—	48
I'll Be Damned	49
Butterfly	50
Broken Promises-	51
Eyes	52
Dust Lust-	53
Good Woman	54
Baby	56
Be To Me As Music	57
The Strong	59
The Bloated Womb	60
Ninny Knew-Nots	61
Blessed Be The Babe	64
The Fall	65
Goose Egg	67
Fat Mama	69
Katherine Scott Florent	71
Black Star	73
Before The End Of Time	75
The Time is Short	77
Garbage Man	81
People Don't Be Meaning What They Say	84
No Matter What They Say	86
Poetic Pleas	87
The Project	88
Mama's Lil Ugly Baby	91
—Sister to Sister	94
Smile	95
People Of The Rain	96
My Mansion	98

Can't Nobody Boogie Like Black Folk	100
That Bone	103
God Bless The Dog	104
Divine Advice	106
Speak It	109
Smile	110
Shame on You, America	113
The Ship	115
I Would Have Been The One	117
This Old Slave	119
Dirty Ole White Man	121
Scars Of Sacrifice	123
Calvary Echoes	125
African Woman	127
Black As I Am	129
To all Mankind-	130
Anyway	131
Carry On	133
Tales Untold	135
An Old New Orleans House	136
A reading from the book of Sirach	138
So Mo Hair Baby	140
I'm Not Really Crazy	143
I Got There	144
My People	145
When The Trumpet Sounds	146
I came	148
Tomorrow	149
Silence	151
This Old Body's Gonna Die	152
Endowment	154
Let Me be a Poet	155

Comfort Zone 157
Hurry, Hurry My Children! translations 159
"Faith Keeper" translations 160
I Want To Go Outside 161
Big Bubba Lil Bubba 164
Mama's Plea 166
A Letter to My Children 169
A Kitchen Woman 172
Age 175
Courageous Men 176
Desiderata 178
Birth Blooming 179
He Speaks 181
My Genealogical History 183
My Heart 188
Nothing Lower 189
Only A Child 190
Problem Solver 191
Shackles 192
They Don't Care 194
Warning 195
Wastin' 196
Waters 197
We Still Stand (After Katrina) 198
Your Big Bald Head 199
Why Retire? 201
Gender Benders 202
"Make Haste My Children!" 204
Still I Smile 205
The Spirit of Joy 207
Quotes From Jeremiah Concerning Life 208

Poetic Works:

Hurry, Hurry My Children!©2010
An Anthology, Book I and Book II
May, I have your Attention Please©1994
Whisper From Within ©1993

Winner of Poster Contest for NAACP, 1970

Books & Publications:

The Tribune Of New Orleans
The Cricket Magazine of New Orleans
American Legion Hall 1987
University of Lafayette Magazine 1994

Louisiana State University
The Daily Reveille
In The Bend of River, & Word Up
—by Kalamu Ya Salaam The Chicken Bones Journal:
African American Periodical

Artistic Works:

Murals of New Orleans Cultural-
(Corner of South Claiborne Avenue and Columbus Street,
New Orleans, LA 70119, circa 2003)
Some Mo Hair Baby
The Gossipers
***Women of NOLA**—Local Broadcasting Cable Network,*
Channel 49, circa 1991
Perseverance Hall, Armstrong Park, 1988 ©

Films:

Women of New Orleans Golden Crayfish 1991,
—Award Winner
Mother of The Ninth Ward Spirit Warriorz

Artistic Performances:

The Neighborhood Gallery
The Universal Thread, with Tim Davis
She is the Root, 1991
Ashe Cultural Center
The Contemporary Arts Center of New Orleans,
1989-1994
New Orleans Public Schools
1990-1999
Delgado University of New Orleans
Xavier University Of New Orleans
Tulane University of New Orleans
Junebug Performance Theater
Word Dance,1996
Ebony Square
Copasetic Community Book Center
Community Book Center
Borsodi's Coffee House

Inroads Internship for Minorities
—St. Louis, Missouri, 1996
Xavier University Graduate
Additional studies at St. Mary's Dominican College

This book is dedicated to Mrs. Zenobia Yolanda Harris

Whose persistence and inspiration led to the completion of this Book. Your Golden years of Wisdom have brought forth new Horizons of awareness . . .

May your diligence in helping to pursue the dreams of others be reflected back to you in an abundance of blessings. Thank you, Lord for this vessel.

Acknowledgements

To my dear and loving parents Percy Jr. and Barbara Darensbourg: Thank you for having given me life and the opportunity to fulfill my uttermost desires and the hopes that you both had for me. And, "Yes," within your saintly state of existence, I hear your applause.

To my husband, Ransom McCormick: Thank you for your patience and giving me support for all of my odd projects, including this book. May we continue to love and tolerate each other until the end of time, also, special thanks for the clan.

To my children:

Rowena McCormick-Robinson and her husband Russell, Tammy McCormick-Broussard and her husband Jarrod, Ransom McCormick and his wife Veda, Percy McCormick and his wife Tameka, Jonah McCormick, Bianca McCormick-Johnson and her husband Jerry, Josiah McCormick and his wife Akira, Damani McCormick, Diarra McCormick, Jeremiah McCormick, Naderah McCormick, Ngozi McCormick and Adesola McCormick

To my siblings:

Sr. Rita Darensbourg SSF, Dolores Darensbourg-White, Don and Joyce Darensbourg, Byron W. Darensbourg, Wanda A. Proctor, Jerome Bias

I would like to express my deepest appreciation to my faithful friend, Ann Washington Cooper, akeia auna leia, who has been a genuine companion to me in the writing of this book. I salute her for always holding me and my work in such high esteem. Without counting the cost in time, effort, or money, Ann has stayed up many hours typing this document. Her sustained support has given me the courage to persevere in getting this book to the finish line. For the blessing of this friendship in action, I am extremely grateful. I roll out the red carpet for her.

Percy and Doris Edwards of Antelope, CA, Darcel Mason, Dorothy Nell Brown, Leola A. Rankins, Michael Stanton, Wanda Stanton, and Mark Edwards

The Darensbourgs, Dixons, McCormicks and Edwards extended family.

Ministry Church Family

The Late Fr. Michael Jacques SSF, St. Peter Claver Church
You commanded the pulpit by bellowing biblical truths and lashing life-learned "I told you so's." You led your flock with soul-stirring charm and galvanized your motivated parishioners for a greater Christian and community good. We will miss your electric persona, fiery speeches, fearlessness and gentle love which are the indelible elements of the legacy you leave behind at St. Peter Claver Church. Your personal connection and love for families has been a great attribute to your character—reflecting that of a saint. Need I say more?

Diane French Cole.
A dedicated community activist whose undying efforts helped to save, direct, and protect our youth through her sacrificial efforts of servitude.

Fr. Jerome LeDoux, S.V.D.
Just your very existence helps lighten life's burdens by knowing your character is still radiating its charisma. Thanks for your non-tiring efforts to reach and embellish the lives of people through your numerous and continuous (over many years) column writing: Louisiana Weekly, The Word, Magazines, etc. Your writings have touched and enriched lives; counseled the youth; unraveled calamity; saved marriages; advised on health; given hope to the bewildered; shed light on ignorance; guided the wayward; broken barriers; accepted the rejected; displayed unending patience; passed on a preserved legacy; and brought chuckles and cheer to the weary-hearted to the max.

Deacon Allen and Edith Stevens of St. Peter Claver Church: remembering to walk by faith
Bishop Levy Q Barnes Jr.: One who glorifies God with song
The Rev. Dr. Vanessa Landry Prelate: Your love for others and passion for the Word will be rewarded.
The Rev. Dr. Marlene Thompson Prelate of Bethel Temple of Deliverance: You are the ship that has rescued many a drifting rafts. Stay on your mission. We need you.

Pastor Gilbert and Joan Singleton of Community Church of God in Christ: Remembering to tell God thank you all the time!
Apostle Darryl G. McCoy of Trumpet in Zion Fellowship: making sure we hear God's message through his powerful delivery Pastor Charles

Garrison of New Genesis Bible Church: saying gospel truths with humor, Hallelujah!

Pastor Eugene and Evangelist Susan King of First Thessalonians Church of God in Christ: exemplifying the Holy Ghost through invincible song and dance.

Minister Doniel Irvin, Vanessa Chavis, Deacon Lawrence Houston, and St. Peter Claver Staff.

Joshua and Sandra Berry Walker: With heartfelt praise and acclaim, I wish to show my appreciation to Joshua and Sandra Berry Walker who allowed the curtain of the Broadway Stage to be drawn back for me. They gave amateur people a chance to perform in the presence of an audience. In the comfortable and cozy surroundings of their Neighborhood Gallery living room, many dormant talents were released by everyday people, discovered and nurtured. Being given a chance at stardom, many venues of opportunity were created for the participants. Thank God for the continuous support in the cultural development of our people.

Zion Trinity: grasping souls by spreading the gospel through rhythm and song.

To Dr. Nana Anoa Nantambu: flaming fire; shooting sparks of wisdom like echoing sounds of homeland awakening and connecting dormant minds.

Fulani Suni-Ali: your knowledge of midwifery blessed my eleventh delivery

Kalamu Ya Salaam: I value your encouragement immensely in remembering your statement, "You write how you write."

Dr. Tayarie Fua Salaam-PHD for remembering your genuine support and consideration for me, an artist/poet, I give thanks. May your blessings flow.

Professor Arthur Pfister: still awaiting Webster's new words to describe your awesomeness.

Chakula Cha Jua: keeping smiling faces in dull places. You are the sun for many a dark spaces.

Carol Bebelle: causing budding flowers to unfold by immersing them in waters of encouragement.

Labertha McCornmick

Queen Jennifer Turner: thank you for being so persistent in your book request from me. It worked!

Vera Warren: for keeping us in tune and connected with historical legacy through the access of books, books and more books. We, the readers, are truly thankful for the enrichment.

Sarah Dave, Margaret Mc Millan, Carolyn Myles, Luther Gray, Mariama Curry, Frozene L. Thomas, Clyde Linda Mathews, Zaydel Clark, Annia Thomas Winn, Dominique B. Wheeler, Valarie T. Saberin, Lucretia Whitley, Karen Sly Strong, Diane Jupiter, Iris Broussard Williams, Debria Washington Harris, Carolyn Craft, Aurolyn McGee, Ann B. Savoir, Gilda Compton Williams, JoAnn Ealy Lemmon, Chalanthia Holloway, Cathy G. Smith, Sandra M. Euwell, Mama Suma and Rhfuaw Diara, Fulami (Julie) Singleton, Mama Efuru J. Alpine, Ifama Diane Arsan, Mona Lisa Soloy, Quo Vadis Gex, Gwendolyn Richards, Samuel Robertson, Jessie Perkins, Olayeelah Daste and Sadi Kaali, Mama Jamila P. Mohammed, Jo Muriel Ojo, Joycelyn Hall Smith, Annie Bell Robertson, Eric and Pamela Johnson, Barbara Taylor Cook, Nilima Mwendo, Ramon Hart, Alice Richardson, Virgie R. Holloway, Dr. Kimberly S. Richards, Zohor and Shaka Zulu, Nathan and Ruth Parker, Sunni Patterson, Regina McCormick-Johnson, Audrey Ann Roy, Myrna Malone, Veronica A. Hunter, Marie Gauthier, Jenella Gibson, Harlo and Elaine Pollar, Alma Woodfork, Wanda and Jerome Williams, Lynn Toval, Rosco Redix, Jr., and Ben Guillory of State Farm, Adisa Adams, Thomas Zuniga, Mary Cecile Thomas, Arnell Robinson, Valentine Pierce, Shirley Clarkson, Alex and Anne Nkenchor, Helene Hemmens, Pro. Cheryl Mckay Dixon, Nyemah Whitfield, Cathleen Lee, Charles Dixon, Westside, New Jersey.

The Booker T. Washington Class of '66

Special dedication to my granddaughter, Jarielle Johnson.

Special thanks to Phoebe Mendoza and Cherry Villa

Now finally, here it is: It's impossible to list everybody. Now I'm running out of time, so here is some extra line sign your own name and put any statement that you want to about yourself. Make yourself sound good now—hear?

Little Old Lady

Reflective to: Mother Theresa

*In her journey of ordinance and love for all,
She walked in obedience and answered her call*

If a little old lady named Theresa changed the world.

Tell me why, why can't we?

*By the tens, by the hundreds, by the thousands
Why?
Why can't we?*

She was flowing with reverence and service to men.

She was filled with holiness that came from within.

**She was just a little old lady
Just a little old lady.
Answering her ordinance
Answering her call.
Just a little old lady**
Just a little old lady
Just a little old lady

A Tribute to Snooks Eaglin

Out of the midst of the abyss of heaven
God stretched forth his hands and created a man
Unique of his kind, and obedient to his call
And God withheld his sight
But intensified his touch and magnified his pluck
And deviated such sound that would gravitate the crowds
Play daddy play
Help big mama dance and shake her cares away
Play daddy play
Ray Charles was a lightening to music,
So is Stevie Wonder
But the music played by Snooks' guitar
Was to them all as thunder
As Domino is to his piano
He was to his guitar
A prodigy extraordinaire, by far, by far
His music was healing to the heart
As well as to your feet, listening to its rhythmic sound
Made it hard to keep your seat
Play daddy play
So we can dance and shake our cares away
Play daddy play
His music was pulsating, you'd just have to juke
To hear the music being played, by the fingers of Master Snook
With amazement he'd pluck on his guitar, with amazement he would sing
And you could move your aching bones
Without feeling any pain.
Play daddy play, take this arthritis in my bones away
Play daddy play
Snook Eaglin was a legend, he taught us all a lot
You don't have to have everything, just use what you got.
What added to his vigor and zest for life was the love and support of his
Devoted wife
He was always in a pleasant mood
His manner was sublime
He plucked away life's problems one guitar string at a time
He's now ascending away into the skies
He's looking down at us smiling
With his brand new pair of eyes
The band in heaven is assembling now
Getting in their right position
You know they'll sound much better
With Snooks as their lead musician
Play daddy play, light up heaven as the angels sway
Play daddy
Play daddy play

Written by: Labertha Darensbourg McCormick

A TRIBUTE TO RUDY

Low swings the chariot
Draped in Kente cloth
The drums beat a homeward sound
For the saint the angel sought.

Low swings the chariot
Draped in Kente cloth
And the angels swing
Open wide God's heavenly doors,
Singing-
He's all the more for God's Kingdom
All the more

And when we find it hard without him
To move on and be at ease
We must remember that it is not good-bye
But-
See you later, Dr. Deteige.

Sacred be the man whose way of life
Brought love and light
To those who may Have been led astray.
Blessed are the youth whose feet had
fortune to trodden in his path.

Dr. Rudolph Deteige
Devoted Principal of Bishop Perry Middle School

Labertha D. MC Cormick
December 29, 2000

Fore-WORD

The Spoken Word

Labertha Theresa Darensbourg-McCormick The writings included in this book stretch throughout a time period of almost 35 years. It has taken over 10 years for me to compile and complete it. Another book will take more time, more organization, preparation, evaluation, concentration, and *time—which is a factor for everyone, whether they realize it or not*. Another book may possibly take me another twenty years.

My readers, we are not guaranteed to witness that span of *time*. So, if you can at all take heed to its contents, I do believe, with certainty, God's inspiration is within it and you will benefit from it in some way. I don't think there is enough *time* left for me to write another one.

My writings reflect back to 1969 when the era of Black pride and awareness was being capitalized and widely dispersed. Through the decades our identified nationality has changed in ethnic titling. We've gone from being called coon to colored, colored to negro, negro to black and black to African American. I resort to using "black" as my identity, simply because it is short, direct, powerful and true. This can be a controversial issue, though it needn't be. There is one race, the human race, and all segments evolve from it: the black race being the corporate, dispersing its fragments of ethnocentricity to all nations.

Henceforth, the poems, *I Am A Black Woman and I'm An African Woman has reference to Africa being the birthplace of all nations (The Mother Land). Thus being so, all nationalities resemble the original race in some way. We are all an African-derived nation*. Don't take my word for it, research your history.

I speak of fragments of my paternal genealogy. Through my research, I have traced my slave given name all the way back to the 17th century on the origin of Darensbourg, a German name. The bearer of this name migrated from a city in Germany (in the 17th century is known as the Arnsberg). It is common knowledge that the slaves bore their owner's name as their property, and you know the privileges of ownership. So here we are, a partial product of whoever our slave masters were, with an inkling of their blood trickling through our veins—be it much little or none (all female slaves did not, of course, bear their masters offspring). For this reason, my German-Creole ancestry does NOT elate me, neither do I give it credence nor shun. It is a historical fact. It is undetermined how many African American people relate to this. It is also a fact that our ancestry all trickles back to AFRICA. Yes we all are a unique people—the offspring of God, destined for royalty.

Furthermore, though continuous historical research, it is documented that my maternal ancestry originated from the coasts of Senegal, West Africa; or from one of the many neighboring cities in Africa. Throughout the continent, during the inhabitants' deportation, it was said that all were channeled through Senegal, a main port city. Cape Verde was also a port city and was given the name "The Port of No Return".

I speak of habitant deportation because in actuality, that was supposed to be the motive. Of the varied information of data gathered, relating to the beginning of the "great expedition of my people" to the US, several truths and related stories have been told.

Initially, one of the stories told, probably true, was that the king encouraged some of his tribe's men to go for great work opportunities as promised, while being, exchanged for goods and commodities, and some went voluntary with fake promises, some as indentured servants, and some were prisoners of tribal wars in exchange for goods. Others were hunted and captured. Here we are, from the port of Senegal to the port of New Orleans.

With communication being primitive, many years elapsed before word got back to homeland that they had become brutally treated slaves, and they were used as catalysts for mass production. As for Cape Verde (another port city), deception, tricker, and greed of free labor had signed its name along its shores as being THE POINT OF NO RETURN.

And for too many years, the inhumane treatment continued. Questions? Do your research. Doubts? Do your research. What a horrific era. Why? Centuries passed until the abolitionists and freedom fighters ended slavery.—though here we are through much suffering, the survivors of the voyage—"the Survivors of the Fittest". A people buffered with resilience, grace, mercy, and the favor of God. Must I remind you? All of us being chosen to be magnificent within our own scope of excellence. Did you know that? You possess an overwhelmingly diverse and rich culture, waiting to be rediscovered and embraced by those who are willing to accept the gifts.

The poetic works of *Ninny-Knew-Not's and Mama's Lil' Ugly Baby* were written around the time of the first half of my family clan of 13 births. Poems like *Fat Mama* and *You're Stuck* were written not only to make homely and so-called "fat" women feel good about themselves, but to engulf them with better satisfaction about themselves; enough to release the old consciousness and latch on to issues of greater importance, such as our final destination.

It is my intention to make you aware of the uniqueness of your given life; and such a gift was not bestowed upon you to be isolated and cloistered into a shell like that of a hermit, but to virtuously blossom and embellish in some way—the lives and purpose of others—with your living fragrance, beauty and fortitude.

If anyone has ever related to you while in the epitome of their trials by saying, "Sista, I been through so much... I could write a book!" Then, the truth in all actuality is—she could write a book if she'd only take the time to do so.

Yes, it is true that everybody has a book, but it is also true that everybody is not going to write one (their own). And within the chapters of one's life, there are parts that are pivotal in excitement and heart—wrenching with deep disappointment, inter-mingled with joy and merriment, tainted with doubt and confusion, support and betrayal, jealousy and deceit, mock and praise, embarrassment and encouragement, and the list goes on and on relating to pros and cons and plain old good and bad news.

It is up to you to decide which of these arenas that you allow to guide your life. Hopefully, I've given an array of hope within some doubtful era of your life's existence, as you juggle with its predicaments. May you be given light to any of your life's circumstances, dilemmas or situations.

In giving humor a lift, you may have a tendency to chuckle at any line or phrase read. As in the poems, *Your Big Bald Head, Calling All Po' Folk, The Project, and That Bone.*

I may lose the thought of being concerned about the reader being offended—and resort to just sounding low-down, ghetto, and derogatory. Sugar-coating or nullifying explicit words would have curtailed the intended message, which is to get you—to act immediately—expecting fast results. As these are crucial times, it requires of us crucial requests, as well as like responses.

There is no nice way to say—"Get this bench off of my foot!" or "Get this tack out of my toe!"

In relating to the piece, "Hurry, Hurry My Children"—our lives are at stake. We must make haste; there is no time to waste.

God's world had a beginning and it will have an ending. My mission is to help make you aware of the apparent approaching Great Transformation (Rapture/ catching away of the Saints).

Although the title, "Hurry, Hurry My Children" was not intended to mislead or confuse you with the contents in relation to children, this book refers to all people, however applicable and thus being so, some choice of words may seem abrasive to some, such as: "Black Star," "Divine Advice" and "Shame On You America." However, there was no other means, as much as I wrestled with words, that I could explain myself and inadvertently speaking cause a reaction. I can be excused, I am not clergy. This being so, several of my poems are related just to children, "Twinkle, Twinkle", "No Matter What They Say" and "Listen to the Elders." I'll leave the copying and separating up to you, for that I didn't have enough time. Inevitably. Much of my writing has nothing to do with my own experiences, but mentally placing myself in the thoughts of others or how I would feel if I were them. All of my writings are from somebody's true experience not being specific as to whom. Everybody can relate to this book in some way or another. Some writings relate to scripture, now do your bible work. I historically associate some of my work to our black past to enrich the readers of our collective black legacy. I give reverence to associated struggles to encourage our youth to appreciate and make use of our freedoms, not to hoard material possessions, or harbor malice and contempt.

I write to bring light to even the lowest of life's circumstances, to bring an array of hope, to the saddest times of our lives of which we all have experienced (that is, if we have lived long enough) and to show hope to the most dire situations that seem hopeless. Though it is my desire to lift one spirit in some way, my style of writing and choices of words don't always bring delight to sensitive ears. Inasmuch as I may have the tendency to view life at a broad or narrow spectrum, a spark of humor is always an antidote. Laughter sustains health and promotes healing. I try to bring spark to that area of our lives where laughter lay dormant.

"For those of you who want to write but can't express yourselves, I write.

For those who try to express yourselves but can't write it so others can read it, I write.

For those who have intentions of writing but never do, I write.

For those who are too intelligent but won't write, I write.

For those who are too envious of me writing this book, I write.

For those who need to be told something that I told them, I write.

For my own satisfaction and through by own disappointment, I write.

For those who have been inspired to write... I won.

Now, write on!"

MEMO LETTER

It is usual that dedications are dedicated to our parents, children or close relatives or friends, because and of course "we love them" and they have a special place in our lives in some in some way or another.

This dedication I present to you is not for the sake of being unusual. Rather, it is necessary for my own satisfaction, as well as the readers. I find it an unpracticed privilege to dedicate this book to—

All the misfits and nitwits, nuts and considered dumb-cluts, outcasts and not appointed, never chosen,

To the lonely and the homely, the forgotten and forsaken, mistreated and mistaken, neglected and rejected, abused and misused, bored and misunderstood,

Fat Mamas, Ugly Babies and The Garbage Men, and those who felt forsaken, and to all my enemies and so-called friends, you have been the inspiration behind the writing of this Book.

I thank GOD for you,

-Your Messenger,
"Mama "Lulu"/ mweka- "keeper"

Hurry, Hurry My Children

Hurry~ Hurry~ My children
For there is a lot to be done and such little time to do it.
Prepare your hearts for the time draweth near."
Really,
The time is up.
The word is out.

He's coming back
This thing is real
Now—what 'chu gonna do about it?

There is no time to take a nap, give a dap, or make a lap.
There's no time for bee-bopping and p—poppin'
Whisker—tweezing and bump squeezing,
Leg shaving and bird—bath—bathing, . . .
Mopping and butt soaking—kissing or reminiscing.

No stroking to the North, South, East Or West
No strolling or belly-rollin', butt shakin' or baby makin'
No time for head scratching or finger tip-tapping,
Rapping or cat nappin'
No time for fumbling, fiddling or finger twiddling.

No time for resting nerves or watching curves
No time for trippin', slippin', fat or skinny-dippin'
No time for making friends or enemies.
Making amends or forgiving sins.

"Hurry, Hurry my children.
The time is up.
the word is out.

Hurry! Hurry My Children

*He's coming back.
This thing is real.
Now—what 'chu gonna do about it?"*

"There's no time for scootin, rootin, tootin or cahootin".

No time for scootin, rootin, tootin or cahootin.
No time for walkin, jumpin, hoppin, humpin or booty bumpin
No time for sittin, spittin, showerin or shi____in.
No time for singin, snortin, burpin and fartin.
No time for wheelin and dealin, chewin and chillin.
No time to blink, wink, bat an eye or think.
No time to chase men, women or dogs.
No time to say grace or feed your face.
No time to sneak, cheat, peek or take a leak.
No time to practice voodoo, hoodoo, cry or boohoo.
No time for hot or cold flashes or batting eyes lashes,
No time for e-mailing or text messaging-
There's no time for counting blessing or giving lessons.
Hurry, Hurry my children

The time is up, the word is out,-
this thing is real.

He's coming back,-

Now, what chu' gonna do about it?

There's no time for frowns smiling faces, or lining teeth with braces
There's no time for feet scraping, finger nail clipping or toe cheese-cleaning.

There no time for match making, or fake jaking,
There's no time for twistin' locks, twirlin' curls or wrappin' naps.

"Hurry, Hurry my children.
The time is up.
the word is out.

LABERTHA McCORNMICK

He's coming back.
This thing is real.
Now—what 'chu gonna do about it?"

"There's no time for scootin, rootin, tootin or cahootin".

There is no time for gripin', fightin', gang—banging, and back bitin'
There is no time for boasting and toasting, braggin' or lolliegagin'
There is no time to even make this poetry rhyme.

There no time to take a smoke, tell a joke, or rock—a boat.
Nor to eat, drink, dream, or think.
There's no time for pouting or doubting,
wailing, whining or monkey-shinin'

No time for attitudes or—*isms*—of any kind,
Hurry, Hurry my children

The time is up, The word is out,
Either you're ready or you're not-

~~~~~~~

Now what chu'....

-Z-O-O-M-M-M!

Where will

You

Fall

Within that Era?

Are you prepared

To

Meet

Your

GOD?

IF's

"IF You let Sin rule in your life,
In time
Every good thing that trys to prevail—
Will be put out like a lightning strike

IF

If you let the devil ride your horse-
He will make you out of a Jackass-

IF

For those women who desire to be police
If you would police at home—
You wouldn't have to police the streets

IF

"If
you don't have an friends
Then…
You aren't a friend
to any."

An excerpt letter

On Education to School Board
1996

"Our children are being lost by the dozens. We have no time to further test the present leadership of this costly institution another year and gamble with their future being indecisive..." is my plea to you "Do something now or everybody loses..."

"It bereaves my spirit to have to deal with this situation, but it also demeans my soul to sit back and 'Watch the good times roll', ...
"To watch it roll on education, dedication and remediation".

> When we wade with the tides,
>   We move smoothly,
> When we wade against the tides
>   We fret and loose stride,
> Wading in the tides
>   Can be success or failure,
> But we first have to have enough courage,
>   To dive into the deep, deep waters—

Cordially,
Mrs. Labertha Darensbourg McCormick Cc/ 6 ro brd. mem.

LISTEN TO THE ELDERS

Listen! To the elders for they are wise.
   They'll teach you how to live and survive.

Listen! To the elders 'cause they've lived a long time.
   They teach you how to make good use of your mind.

Listen! To the elders and if you do; you have a long
   and good life too.

Listen! To the elders and as you live your life;
   you'll find out that the elders were right.

If you will . . .
   Listen, to the elders
      Listen, to the elders
         Listen, to the elders

In 1996, Father Michael Jacques came to the aid of a church, St. Phillip the Apostle, struggling to stay open and was successful in his efforts.

Hurried Help

Expediently you came to a church that was in dwindle
Expediently you worked so our church would rekindle

Exceptionally you performed your duty as God intended
Humbly you restored the joy as differences were mended

Wonderfully you pulled together those who were foreign to each other
Feverishly you worked all your human strength was worth

Sacrificially you paved a way that's memorable to our church
Unselfishly you gave to the degree surpassing

Truthfully you showed a love, true and everlasting
Deeply you got involved to troubleshoot and trouble solve

Remarkably you reached the peak of your performance
Sincerely you showed us how to keep the faith and have endurance

Grand Ma's Feet

* * *

- ❖ Grandma's Feet be a sacred thing.
- ❖ Grandma's feet be sore from strain.
- ❖ Grandma feet be relieved again, when you rub'em

Now, if you've got a Grandma's feet to rub, you'd better rub'em.
      Rub them firm to circulate the flow-
      Of blood that goes from her bones to your very own.
Rub them firm to circulate the flow of blood the goes from her tippy-toes to her finger-tips, to her smiling lips.

Rub them firm to hold onto the last of the sacred past.

Feet that stood besides the ironing board and ironed all day til they were
    aching sore.
Feet that stood and worked all day for white folks' measly pay.
Feet that took for you your forward steps, till you could step yourself,
Feet that cleared for you a path of vines, until a path you'd find.

Feet whose arms would hold you on her knee and try to comfort thee-

Just take the time to do a deed that's kind

Time's unwinding and moving on
      Don't doubt what I say,
        Just look around and see-

The Grandma's feet~~~
      That's goooooone.

If you've got a Grandma's feet to rub~~~
      Rub—'em.

LDM © 1995

HEALING POWERS

We all have healing powers.

They are in our minds, our moods, our words, our ways,-
Our positive attitude, our sharing of gratitude-
Powers—
Healing powers.

They are in our signs, our song, our touch,
Our good rapport with people, as such
Our smile, our hugs, our just being nice,
And in doing things that show self—sacrifice,
And the power is free. There is no price-
Powers that heal, powers that heal.

They are in our love, that show we care.
They are in our open arms of welcoming warmth.
They are in our prayers.

Powers that heal, powers that heals.
Let us all project to each
Other—our healing powers and
Heal one another—heal one
Another-

Labertha McCormick ©(1993 whispers

SPEAK EASY

Don't let your tongue be a dagger to whomever you may speak.
Just speak easy, easy, and let you choice of words be meek.
     Speak Easy~ *easy*—
So that the words you bring won't be a sting to someone else's ear.
So that the message that is shouted out won't reach the one not meant to hear.   Speak Easy~*easy*—

So that the cursing words that we blurt out won't cause us to be in sin.
And bitter thoughts that's in our minds, are sometimes better left within.

Speak *e-a-s-y.*
So that the words that should be whispered, won't come out in a shout,
'Cause you know that what's shouted out be hardly worth one hearing about,
And considering to take words back is an im-pos-si-bil-ity

So speak, *easy*, speak *easy* . . .

Now easy is to compromise as bitter is to scold,
And within our hearts we should control the thoughts that could be as console.
Speak easy—
So that the bad thoughts that might blurted out, would have a chance to flee,
So that the evil thoughts that's hollered out, would have the chance to cease.
Speak easy—
You know the angered words that you shout out, be better left unsaid,
And regretting what you shouted out, you won't later have to dread, If you just—Speak easy...

So that's what's bursting up inside you, may have a chance to cool, because the language of an angered mouth is like that of a fool... So *speak easy, easy, speak easy.*   (Proverbs 12:18)

We are tough-
Quite enough
Made from—"GOOD STOCK"-

Come from GOOD STUFF-

We are treasures—true creations of God

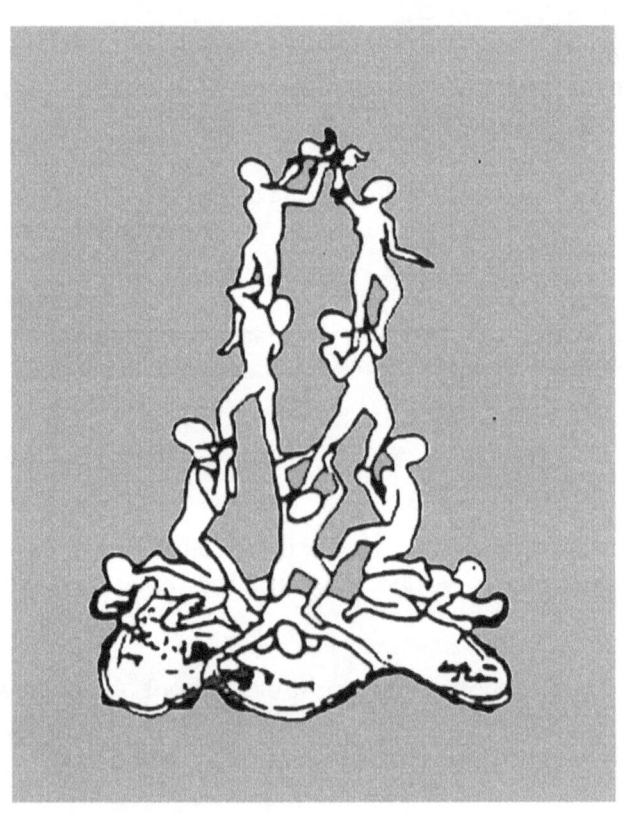

"Each one lifts One..."

The sooner you accept your *uniqueness*
In the image
Of
Almighty *God*
In the image he
Has made you
The better you *will feel* about *yourself*
The more *you will do* for yourself
And
Everybody else
Behold
Your own beauty

Nappy Headed

I got tired of being nappy-headed, breaking combs and bending picks, and curling brush bristles through hard labor.
I got tired of being nappy-headed, nappy-headed nappy-headed.
I got tired of aching elbows and wearing my arms out just to be socially accepted.
I just wanted my hair to be straight so when I'd turn my head, it would slap me in the face.

I got tired of dealing with the chinchi-binchies.
I just wanted my hair to grow straight from the roots, loose and bouncy.
I just didn't want to be nappy-headed, nappy-headed, nappy-headed.
I got tired of committing my time, my life my hair to hot combs and chemicals.

The hot comb will straighten the naps away for a day-or two, but if its one degree too hot it will comb and burn your hair away for months and Sundays.

The relaxer is fine if you' be got your money on time, or that new growth of naps will over-rule the straights and you'll have a bad case of the breaks and be picky-headed.
The costly curls is fine, provided that you continuously slop and sop your head with the curl m-o-i-s-t-u-r-e—a—c-t-i-v-a-t-o-r.
     But
Don't step right out in the~~ Cold.
Or
"you'll catch the walking pneumonia of the black folks brain."

Don't think that just because your hair grows straight or wavy from the roots,
That your off-spring is free from being nappy-headed.
The chances are when genes show through, babe might be born with the chinchi—binchies because if you're black, somebody, somewhere down long the line was nappy-headed.

Don't think that just because your hair grows wavy from the roots and you only get a mild relaxer, cause anytime you spend the same amount Of money on a mild relaxer; as you do for and extra strength for nappy-naps You'd just as well be just as nappy-headed

All the time I spent trying not to nappy-headed, I could 'a done got myself some more E-d-u-c-a-t-i-o-n.
All the money I spent trying not to be nappy-headed, could' a been donated to some homeless dude.

So, I tried this stuff invented by Concerned Individuals for Kink-Conscious Individuals to make my hair grow out straight fro the roots, assuring me of no more chinchi-binchies, no more being nappy-headed. Then three months went by and there was no sign of those unruly snatch-back chinchi—binchies.
Three months had gone and there was no sign of hair, anywhere Now six months have gone and my prayers is that:
"I please have some sign of hair."
~~~~~~

Just a few nice naps, some cool kinks, some wiry wool, some truly unrulies, Never mind if its bad, any kink is good,

Let it be cucka-bucks, if you don't mind, even snatch-backs will do."

Don't need no big old 'fro How about a few chinchi-binchies, a few cucka-bucks, knotty knots, or even little locks.
Yeah, that'll work, that'll work.
Just enough just to make me nappy, nappy, nappy-headed.

LDM © 1988

LABERTHA McCORNMICK

COMMON WOMAN

I'm a common woman,
Common is the name I bear
While some folk worry about keeping up with the Joneses
I just don't give a care.

I'm a ommon woman,
Walking on common grounds
'preciating all things of commonness around to be found

I'm a common woman,
No matter how fancy I appear to be,
I could give up all these fancy things and be just common me.

My comfort is barefoot toes on hard wooden floors
That's gonna bring me closer to the ground.
My comfort is loose-fitting clothes and no pantyhose.
That way I keep my commonness profound.

I'm a common woman
Who lives the common cause
Don't need no fancy lace panties to cling to my fanny
Just give me some dirt cheap common drawers.

I'm a common woman and common is when I'm at my best
Don't need no glitter toes
And rolls and fros on clothes of which I dress.
Don't need no shoulder-length hair to look debonair
Or fill me with delight,
Just give me an inch—and it'll be a cinch
To make me think I'm out of sight.

I'm a common woman
Whose plain and fancy freed
Don't need no rigmaroles and sassy time
Clothes to meet my common needs.

Don't need no make-up on
To make me look like one of those clown-faced model
chicks, I wash down my face and slick down my brows with
my own natural make up-spit.

I'm a common woman, being common as
I emphasize, Don't need no jingles, jangles and
jewelry that tangles to make my spirits rise.

Don't need no false eyelashes and clothes
That flashes to give my soul a lift,
Don't need no holiday folly by spending your money
On some expensive gift.

Common woman,
Don't need no tight fittin' jeans as one of means
To show my feminisque, no certain code is gonna set the mode
For the common kinda way I dress 'cause
I'm a common woman.

Don't need no air-conditioned room
To take away the gloom and my temperature
right, just give me a ceiling fan and a cool-hand
man and I can make it through the night.
Don't need no birth control method to set
My record on how I need to conceive
Don't need no soap opera shows to tell me
How life goes, or in what I need to believe.

I'm a common woman who lives by common accord
And I'm superseding simply by the biblical word of my Lord.

I'm a common woman,
With a common kinda, common kinda warmness

LABERTHA MCCORNMICK

And a common kinda, common kinda longingness
For a common kinda, common kinda, common kinda caress.

With a common kinda, common kinda
Hugging and a common kinda
Common kinda loving
Cause these are things of commonness
I'm a common woman, O yes, I'm a common woman
Uh-Huh—I'm a common woman
I'm a common woman kinda, common kinda, cooooommon woman—

You're Stuck

Oh, you're stuck baby, you are stuck. You're stuck baby, you are stuck.
Oh, you're stuck baby, you are stuck.
You're stuck baby, you are stuck.
It ain't no need of you worrin bout tryin' to hold those big lips in, just because you want to be thin-
Cause you're stuck baby, You're stuck with that.
Ain't no need you worrin' bout trying to close-pin that big nose just because it's covering too much space across your face, cause baby! You are stuck with that.
It ain't no need of you worrin' bout tryin' to make that nappy hair fly fluff and go straight without hot combs or chemicals because You're stuck baby, you are stuck with that.
it ain't no need of you worrin' about tryin' to change one of the many shades of blacks to the one and only white, because you're stuck with that
It ain't no need of you worrin' bout putting a cap on that gap cause you happen to be one of the s-p-a-c-e teeth sisters because You're stuck baby, You're stuck with that.
It ain't no need of you worrin' bout trying to bind that behind, Just because you may happen to be one of the "Butt Sisters" Because you're sure enough stuck with that.
It ain't no need of you worrin' bout trying to change those Black-brown eyes to any shades of blue eyes because You are stuck baby, stuck with that.
It ain't no need of you worrin' bout trying to add meat to those legs alone, Just because they happen to be skin and bones,
To change that size 11 shoe just because you don't want it to belong to you, To hold back the rhythm, that your body has "got to give 'em" To hold back the boogie when your body wants to woogie, To control that "soul" that your body's got on hold.
It ain't no need of you tryin' to change black to white,
Don't you know you're already out of sight?
So be glad to be,

Be obliged to be,
Be
F L A T T E R E D to be stuck baby, stuck with that,
'Cause you're stuck baby, Stuck with that.
Be in a hurry to be glad to be stuck!
Labertha D. McCormick©1986

I am fearfully and wonderfully made Psalms 139: 14

I am the BLACK WOMAN

I Am the Birth Mother of all nations, of firm and
—African foundation.
I am the Black Woman.
I am the master stroke of mother wit . . .
I am the master key of maternal love I am the tough-bellied child bearer.
I have no fear to persevere. I am eccentric, I am the Black Woman.

I am the pyramid of femininity
I am the epitome of womanhood
I am an hour glass . . .
I am the profound edifier of comfort
I am the bearer of family infirmities
I am the gold fist and tender fingers.
I am blood-blasting! Bold! Long—lasting!!!
I am the Black—Woman.

I'm like a live locomotive with the power of a workhorse.
    -backed by the stamina of being a Black Woman.

I am a non-tiring ball-firing
I am a load carrier and burden bearer.
I am a brain user and defeat refuser
I am a non-slower on-goers,

I am everybody's mama and my own toilet cleaner.

I am the head rag tied intellectual,
-with the tolerance of a tiger-tamer.

I am the griever, moaner, crier, self-healer, self—riser.
    I am the Black Woman.

Labertha McCornmick

I am the family's chorus and the lonely man's song,
I am the antidote to a weary man's woes.
I am the heart beat of my household.
I am the 8 to 4 and a 4 to forever.
    There's not a task for me that I won't endeavor
I am the Black Woman.

I nurtured my own young and some of everybody else's—
I am the ninny, the nanny, the mama, the mammy,
The papa, the mau, the annie, the granny.
I am the Black Woman.
Does anybody know me?

I am a pain tolerator and a self determinator.
I am the episode of an undying era.
I am the legacy of a matriarch.
I am the backbone, the shoulder blade and the rib cage of my off—springs.
I am the Black Woman.
Does anybody know me?

I am a prayer knee bender and a bo-bo mender
I am the doctor, the housekeeper,
the nurse, the bread bringer-

    I am the Black Woman.
        Does anybody know me?

I am a home economizer and a self sacrificer
I am a fish frier and meal multiplier.
I am a home remedia and a self rejuvenator.
I am the Black Woman.
I am the master spring against hard times.
    I am the Black woman.
        Does anybody know me?

I nurtured my own young and some of everybody else's
I am the ninny, the nanny, the mama, the mammy,
the papa, the mau, the annie, the granny.

*I am the Black Woman.
Does anybody know me?*

*I am the 8 to 4 and a 4 to forever
I am the 8 to 4 and a 4 to forever
    I am the 8 to 4 an a a 4 to forever*

*There's not a task for me that I won't endeavor.
    I am the Black Woman
        Does anybody know me?*

Labertha D. McCormick©1989

WHAT SHOULD I TELL MY CHILD WHOSE HEAD IS LONG?

I'd tell him that when he was born the angels swarmed around his bed—admiring one of God's newest creations, admiring too—his big long head.

What should I tell my child whose head is long?
I'd tell him—To ignore the tease of youngsters who do not know why God made him so remarkably different, but distinctively in the image of God Himself.

What should I tell my child, whose head is long?
I'd tell him that his big long head serves as a halo to his face, who's smile is a tribute to the sun, that lightens every darkened place.

Now, who would even question or dare dispute the craftsmanship of God's designing hands?

What should I tell my child, whose head is long?
I'd tell him that his big long head serves as a haven to his brain and has more room then to expand his wisdom and his genius.

What should I tell my child whose head is long?
I'd tell him that his big long head serves as a shell, and his brain is protected twice as well.

I'd tell him to just look around, and see the world so beauty bound, with heads big, little, long, square and round, all created so perfectible with flaws so undetectable.

Now, who would even question the efficiency of God's designing hands?
I'd tell him that his big long head is artistically carved and meticulously shaped and by no means is a mistake.

*Not even a fool would dare
dispute the craftsmanship
resulting from the mighty
works*

*-wonderfully done
by
God's designing hands.
That's what I'd tell my child,
-whose head is long.*

(Written for Damani, my long-headed and handsome son), 1984

MY CHILD

I want you to know you are sufficient in yourself.
Though you may not make headlines in your attempts for success
Though you may not gain high acclaim in trying to do you best, My child you are sufficient.

Though your beauty may not capture the eyes that beauty seekers seek, You are sufficient in the eyes of your creator, You are sufficient and complete.

The word sufficient may seem meager with or without the test; but it is the meaning of a high achiever; when you've done your very best.

Listen, my child if within your utmost effort, sufficient be you score; that sufficient is, as sufficient does, amply supplies, plus gives a little more.

       I want you to never feel, my child that you are deficient
       In any form within yourself.
Just press forward knowing and feeling and believing that you my child, are sufficient.

LAZY BOY

You lazy boy, you lazy, lazy, lazy boy.
With that straw stuck in yo' mouth,
With them legs crossed together.
With that big weaved hat on yo' head.
sittin' there reading that paper.

Don't you know you is a lazy boy?
But I tell you one thing you better git up before
them white folks think You a crazy boy, crazy,
crazy, crazy boy

—Rowena McCormick
Age 9—1982

A SHUCK TIME POET

Oh, I'm just a shuck-time poet,
Who's just a shuckin' with the time,
Writing straight from my emotion,
Writing straight from my mind.

Oh, I like using my bad English,
And colloquial quotes, feeling free-talking trash,
But
Even when I'm serious, It comes out like a joke.
I be just shuckin', I be just shuckin'

Never published a poem
But be good if I could
And even if I do or don't
My poetry be good,
Cause it uplifts my spirits,
And is good for my mind,
It's like I'm telling you,
      I'm just a shuck—time poet, shuckin' time.*

(c) 1979

NO TIME FOR POETRY

Ain't nobody got no time to listen to no poetry.

Don't nobody care about why the red sun sat behind the hills of afternoon.

Ain't nobody got no time to listen to no poetry

They could find some time to listen to some poetry.
But they are just living on the everyday stride trying to stay alive.

They could find some time to listen to some poetry.
They just don't want to admit
That they are **J—I—V—E**

_____

(c) 1981

Labertha McCornmick

A NICE PARTY

I invited them to my party but didn't nobody come.
Didn't nobody come even though I told them it would be a nice party with nice food and no additives; all good for your health with no preservatives,

I had good food and no meat
Healthy snacks and no sweets,
Nice air with no mari-aroma

It was goanna be a nice party, but didn't nobody come.
I was even goanna have some nice music for good vibrations, with nice lyrics and no vulgar connotations. Nice dance with no Solid Gold gestations. It was goanna be a nice, nice party but didn't nobody come. Now I was even goanna have some nice wine, the kind they serve with holy communion.
No hard stuff.
I was goanna have a nice atmosphere with no loud cussing, with no too-tight pants and no two-timer talk.
E v e r y t h i n g was goanna be nice.
I invited them to my party, but didn't nobody come.
Now, tell me? Do you think, that was nice?

(c) 1986

CALLING ALL PO' FOLK

LaBertha D. McCormick©1984
CALLING ALL PO'FOLK
Calling all Po' folk
Not everybody know that they are po' folk but
If you scuffle to catch a quarter before it rolls into the gutter
Then
You're a po' folk-
If you ride till the tank's on "E" ~

but
when you gas up
You just spend three
Then
You're a po' folk.
If you raid the clearance rack, and when you
Check out you have a stack
Then
you're a po'folk.-
If you leave food for public's sake, but
When At home, you lick the plate
Then
You're a po' folk.-
If you bring home a doggie bag
But
when you get home, its your tail that wags
Then you're a po' folk.-

Hey, you growling-belly business brief case carrier, don't you know you're a Po' folk? Hey, you tight-wad penny-pincher. Don't you know you're a po' folk? Ah! Po' folk live a mighty long time—
Without a dime!*

(c) 1985

"I AIN'T GOT NOBODY..."

I AIN'T GOT NOBODY
LbM©1987

Hey, you over there, you can come by me,
Cause I ain't got nobody.
Don't let this belly fool you, it's just a front.
Looks like I had somebody, but I ain't got nobody now.
Nobody.

My man's done gone . . . yeah.
My man done skip city cross my belly.
I ain't heard from him since he heard 'bout this baby.
That's no way to treat a lady in love.
Now I know that he was jive, by I 'da never thought he'd c—o-n-n-I-v-e me this way.
And he knowed I wanted to get married while I could still squeeze into one of them cute little wedding gowns.

*He knowed I 'da made him a good wife,
Cause I'm a easy lover, You could see that, and a fast cook.
I used to dish him up a can of pork and beans and pork chops, all in ten mintues.
After I asked him to legalize our shacking since I was shaping into a mama,—*

He told me he didn't even much know he could make no babies.

Now you know he was wrong for that.

*He told me, afte-r knocking me up, that I was the one making a big thing out of nothing-
Now, you know he was wrong for that.
He told me to go to your friends for support, cause that's what friends are for. Now you know he done me wrong.*

*Left me all alone.
Do that sound like I got somebody?
Do that sound like I got somebody to you?
I ain't got nobody.
I ain't got nobody but me and I'm getting tired of it
being just me that I see.*

*The only sign I got now of a man is proof that I done had one.
How could a man leave a good woman this way?
Somebody, Oh, somebody, wont cha come by me and maybe we could go dining at McDonald's or dancing at the "Dungeon" while I can still do a disco.
Just offer me some simple companionship.
I should not have to be by myself with a shape like this.*

*Mr. Young Man,
Mr. Old Man,
Mr. Nobody—
I need somebody to come by me.
Mr. Cool Man, Mr. Clean, or even Mr. T.
Somebody from somewhere needs to come by me.
Cause I ain't got nobody.*

LABERTHA McCORNMICK

Nobody.
So, somebody won't you please come by me?
Hurry!

"Just forgive the sucka, forget the sucka—and live a wonderful life."
"Be in a hurry to say 'no' to a quick decision"

THE LUCKY ONES

Some things in life are not to be shared.
Some things in life are made just for One
—Such things as:
One Plum—for one someone.

Now, that I have 13 children
And only 5 plums,
Someone will do without
To share these plums with bites and spits from different ones would spread countless germs.
Therefore- someone will not taste the sweet bitterness of these 5 plums

While, being very discreet,
I will issue to 5 chosen children.

Chosen for the moment are the ones who will eat them
Also, secretly—they are—for the moment "The Lucky Ones"

Yes, these plums are for "The Lucky Ones"

Some things in life are not to be shared.—

Lbc2000(c)

LABERTHA McCORNMICK

THE WIND

It don't too much matter now,
What they say—cause
The worst is done now and my soul
-has some recuperation to do,
My heart some slowing down.

-"Ring around Rosie"—is for kids
and just what's for me is yet to be known.

What they say is just the millionth repetition of past episodes,
To the new occupants of that time.

What they say is like the wind, the wind that moves against you when you move.

That moves against you when you are still.

It don't too much matter now what they say cause what they say, is like the wind.
Be in a Hurry to remember this.

TWINKLE, TWINKLE

Twinkle, twinkle little African stars.
You no longer have to wonder who you are.
You are a people of African descent,
Who many a year in slavery was spent.

You are the descendants of ingenious kings,
With blood of royalty flowing in your veins.
You are descendants of intelligent queens,
Capable of accomplishing marvelous things,

You are a people of great contribution,
Who through many a problems gave helpful solutions.

Twinkle, twinkle, litte African stars
You no longer have to wonder who you are
You are a people through whom desecration has sprung,
Like a rose growing in the desert sun.

You are a people in spite of slavery scars,
Have managed to be the genuine person you are and don't let nobody
And don't let nobody tell you you can't do it.
Go on, be a doctor, be a lawyer, just put your mind to it.
You are a people of spiritual mind,
Who has maintained the ability to overcome the bind
So, go out into the world and build on our nation.
You are our present ideals; over future generations.
And remember, your shine is throughout the universe,
Your glow is seen from afar

Twinkle, twinkle African stars.
A marvelous kind of people is who you really are.
Be your best
Be a star—Hurry!

(c) 1983

—WALK—

*Cautiously away from
What looks like trouble
But
If by chance
You find yourself
In the midst
Of what you know is trouble
Immediately
Learn to fly!!!*

I'LL BE DAMNED

You come from two daddies,
One Black and One white,
That's why you two brothers,
Look like a day and a night.
Now, neith—eeeeeeeeeer one of them is here,
To break up a fight, and to disown one another
In no way is what's right.

I'll be damned if you disown your brother.
You sucked the same titty, come out the same hole.
Ate out the same plate, licked the same bowl.
Played in the same dirt.
Wore the same shirt.
Ate out the same lunch bag, Wiped snot from the same snot rag.
I'd be damned if you disown your brother.

You peed in the same bed,
Crapped in the same commode.
Used the same tooth brush,
Wore the same clothes.
Sat on the same lap, shared the same cap
Used the same shoes

Shared the same blues
Come from the same background.
You're mother same and brother bound.
There ain't another brother around to be found, and
I'll be damned if you disown your brother,
More then damned if you disown your brother

(c) 1982

LABERTHA MCCORNMICK

BUTTERFLY

TO YOU YOUNG WOMAN,
I GIVE THIS ADVICE.
TREAT YOURSELF AS IF YOU ARE
A BUTTERFLY IN FLIGHT.

DISPERSING YOUR BEAUTY AS
YOU FLOAT IN GOD'S ATMOSPHERE

WHILE ADRIFT, STAY SWIFT FOR IF YOU LAND ON HIS EGO,
HE MAY TRY TO CAPTURE YOU AND DAMAGE YOUR WINGS
IT WILL BE AS IF HE
STUCK HIS FINGERS IN A SPIDER'S WEB...
IMPOSSIBLE TO REPAIR.
YOU ARE AS THE BUTTERFLY,
TO BE ADMIRED AND NOT TOUCHED.

ONLY VOWS MAKES YOUR CAPTURE A
SACRED THING.

BE IN A HURRY, YOUNG WOMAN, TO GUARD YOUR CHASITY.

Labertha MCCormick ©1985

BROKEN PROMISES-

You promised me sweet happiness.
That one day my heart be filled.

You promised me a wedding band.
That my ring finger would fill.

You promised me, Oh, you promised me
All kinds of sweet thrills.

You promised me a baby, too
which was my heart's desire.

But no ring, no band, no happiness
Has left my heart on fire.

Now I have no man to dress my ringless hand.
-So lonely be my heart for you.
-And lonely be my belly, too

_____
(c) 1975

EYES

Eyes tell other eyes
That the mouths of each others eyes,
Tell lies.
But
Eyes alone bare no falsity.

Tongues may speak,
Hands may do,
And bodies may perform,
The actions of lies,
But
Eyes bare unspoken words,
Never to be heard,
Only known, by eyes alone,

Mouths may form that crescent smile
For each others satisfaction.
Hands may give the traditional shake,
As a spontaneous reaction.
Bodies may turn their backs on each other,
After their mouths told lies.
But
The thoughts of the eyes
Whose mouths told those lies,
Never dies . . . cause
Eyes tell other eyes
That
The mouth of each others eyes,
Tells lies.

Lbmc©1990

Dust Lust-

From dust you are
a n d
      t
    o
          D
            U
              S
                T

you
   shall
      return.

    This is a fact, my man, that you need to learn.
    I see that fire in your eyes when all that flesh
    Goes rolling by, but that big behind that you're spying is just dust in your eyes. Just a hunk of dust, my darling, or shall I say two.
    Enough dust to fill up a bucket when all the living is through. Why put yourself in jeopardy for that you cannot claim?
    Cause when it boils down to the nitty gritty, the results are just the same.
    So go on, my darling, lust if you must, just remember that the fact remains,
    You're just lusting after dust.

    LBMcCormick

(c) 1983

GOOD WOMAN

It seems like somebody ought to want to take a good woman; just for the sake of having a good woman.
All because she's a good woman.
Seem like somebody want to say-
"Hey, good woman,"
Come my way, good woman
Or
"Make my day good woman . . ."
All because she's a good woman.

It seems like somebody ought to want to grab a good woman; just to have a good woman.
All because she's a good woman.
Seem like somebody out to want to meet a good woman; just to treat a good woman.
All because she's a good woman.

It seems like somebody ought to want to run down a good woman; to be round a good woman—
All because she's a good woman.
It seem like somebody would want to hold a good woman; just to console a good woman—
All because she's a good woman.

It seems to me like a good man ought to find a good woman all because he's a good man and she's a good woman.
And she's a good woman.
Oh, but what it seems—
What it seems-

Ends in nothing but what
  ONE DREAMS-
But—
  That's what it SEEMS like—
    anyway.

BABY

Baby, you know I love you, Baby
You know you'll always be my Hoochie Coochie Man.
Baby, you know I love you, Baby
And I don't want nobody
Messing with my tu-tu
Messin with my sweet.
Messing with my boo.
Don't want nobody messing with my—
BABY!
You know I love you, Baby,
And I don't want nobody
Messing with my mancho
Messing with my muse.—
Don't want nobody messing with my
Baby, You know I love you, Baby
When the sun comes up in the morning—you bees on my mind.
When sun goes down in the evening—you bees on my mind. Everywhere and all the time.
You bees on my mind, Baby

You bees on my mind, Baby
And I don't want nobody
Messing with my ya-ya
Messing with my tussi
Messing with my fire.
Baby—all my love for you I'll save
You know, I got the kind of love for you that I'll carry to my grave.
Baby, You know I love you, baby How mo' can I say so, Baby?

LDMc©1990

Taken from the skit, "One and Only" (c) 1982

Be To Me As Music

Be to me as music
Be to me as music to my ear
And sweep that melancholy mood away.

Be to me as a comfort to my soul
And let life's drudgery pleasantly unfold.
Be to me as music, music to my ear.

Be to me as a sweet serenade
Surrounding me in gaiety.
Bring charm to me as a bird's melody
Enchanting to my soul.

Just be to me as music,
Be to me as music to my ear
Be to me as music, music to my ear.

Be to me as a loving man whose worth the hugging,
Be to me as music, music to my ear.

Engulf me with sweet promises,
that are never to be broken.
And let it be as music to my ear
each word to me that's spoken.

Be to me as music,
Be to me as music to my ear,
Be to me as music, music to my ear.
Be to me as ethics to a song,
And let the blues then be forsaken,
And let my spirits fly to the highest

LABERTHA MCCORNMICK

Pitch of satisfaction.

Be to me as music,
Be to me as music to my ear,
Be to me as music, music to my ear.

And sweep that melancholy mood away.

THE STRONG

Nobody knows the tears of
The strong
They cry in solitude
The cry alone
So when they go among the croud
Their tears are all gone
Seldom do we see
The tears of the strong

THE BLOATED WOMB

Low be to the man who cursed the woman with the bloated womb.
    Pity be to his person
    Shame to his name.

Through the womb of a woman you came,
Through the womb of a woman in pain you came.
Though she may not be the woman from whose womb you came
The pain of that woman is much the same.

The bloated womb of a woman has pain.
Your life was not given to utter such shame.
Your life was not given to mock with blame.
Low, be the man who cursed the woman with the bloated womb.
    Pity to his person
    Shame to his name.

NINNY KNEW-NOTS

Ahh!~ Who knows the lady whose baby whose baby
knew not the ninny.
For too many, too many knew not the best, knew not the ninny.
For the new born baby, give up the ninny while there plenty to give him.
Give him plenty and lessen the quest for the cancerous breast.
-For that which is not used will deteriorate.

Woe, Woe to you lady, to you lady
Whose baby, whose baby knew not the ninny;
For in a generations to come, there won't be any.
Not a bulge, not a tit,
Nothing left to resemble a ninny; from the womb to the tomb.
—Too many, too many, knew not the best, knew not
the breast, knew not the ninny.
I'm not talking to you, little ladies who couldn't-
I'm talking to you smart, cute lady, with a baby, *who wouldn't, cause she couldn't* . . .

Woe, woe to the lady, to the lady whose baby knew not the ninny. So smart you claim to be, to hold back the ninny, and nurse your yearning new-born from a cow, goat or guinea.
But even the kneel down to the needs of their young.
    How could you deny the best and don't give him none?

Your newborn need not be clung to the milk of a cow, no more than a newborn calf need be clung to the milk of a lady.
    -*Need not you wonder the occurrence of the wild child.*

LABERTHA McCORNMICK

~~~~~~~~~~~~~~~~~~
Woe, woe to you lady, to you lady
Whose baby, whose baby, know not the ninny

OH,- but there's the man who gets the ninny,
—for him there's two.
For the baby, not any.
Now, if you really don't know,
What God gave you ninnies for,
Watch the dog with her pups,
Watch the hog with her pigs,
Watch the goat with her kids,
Watch the tree climbing monkey,
They know, they know.

If you could read the language of the 4-legged,
As they watch you drain and rob their titty bags,
You'd hear them heckling and he-hawing at you humans.
For getting no more use out of your ninnies,
Then to fill out a 34 B titty—strap by Maidenform.

Need you miss what might be your only change in life time to feel the touch of a tiny baby's tiny mouth.

Splendid is the touch, as splendid as the touch of the hand of Mary to the baby Jesus.

Glorious is the touch, as glorious as the touch of the toe of Jesus to the River Jordan.

AH! ~Don't be the lady, whose baby, know not the ninny.
Far too many, too many knew not the best, knew not the breast, know not the ninny.
Now, take heed to this plea,

AHH!—for as generation, from generation shall pass
There'll be no more ninnies, no ninny,
Just
       ASS!

Labertha McCormick©1986

Remember- one who laughs- lasts.

BLESSED BE THE BABE

Blessed be the babe laying in the manger
Blessed be the way He came
Blessed be the angels who swarm around Him
Blessed be His holy name.

Blessed be the Kings who from afar have traveled,
Blessed be the country men who came and marveled
Blessed be the animals who gave Him warmth

Blessed be the elders who tell the story.
Blessed be the people who live for His glory.
Blessed be the holy way He came,
Blessed be the babe who is called Jesus
Blessed be His holy name.

Blessed be the children who are willing to listen!
Blessed be those whose lives are Christian
      Amen

LBMc1992

THE FALL

Let me be worth falling from my mother's womb
Let me be worth the pain of her labor.

Let every breath I take be counteracted
by a deed for someone.
Let my spirit be exuberating for all.

May someone's heart be lifted
because of me.
May someone's heart benefit
because of my being.
Then least I be worth falling from my mother's womb.
Least
I be worth the pain of her labor.

The pain is in the labor, but the being be worth the fall.
So let them be worth the fall.

So let them fall, women-
Let them fall-
Let them fall-

*"Covering up Truth
Is
worse than putting a bandage
over
Embedded Glass."*

Goose Egg

So, you sit there on your goose egg with self-glorification, satisfied, bubbling over with self-contained, self-contentment...
Waiting for your *"forever coming"—tomorrow so you might even bulge;*
    While you sit there in your coop
Hovering over your goose egg, with the self-contained philosophy:
    "I ain't' goanna bother no-body,
    So no-body please don't bother me."

Folks just pass you by—in need of your help, in need of your concern,
You don't want to help nobody cause you're scared you might get tired.
You don't want to do no good deed cause you scared you might get too s-a-n-c-t-l-m-o-n-l-o-u-s.

You, Don't want to share nothing!
"CAUSE YOU'RE JUST A STINGY SOMEBODY!
Yeah,
—while you sit there waddling with self-contentment, scared to raise your behind from over your goose egg, your tomorrow is forever coming your product is nothing, your goose egg ain't nothing but air.
    ~And you ain't nothing but a jive—chump—on a lump!
Be in a Hurry to get off your goose egg
Labertha MC Cormick © *Whisper from Within 1993*

I am fearfully and wonderfully made Psalms 139: 14

Fat Mama

Fat Mama wanted to lose weight.
Fat Mama really tried.
Fat Mama went on a crash diet
And liked to died.
Fat Mama did some of this and some of the other-
Fat Mama couldn't seem to do nothing to shed that blubber.
But Fat Mama didn't sit on the steps a sobbing.

Fat Mama rolled that fat together and went a flobbing,

Fat Mama was huge and voluptuous, needless to say how rumptious-
Fat Mama primped and pampered and did what she could and you can bet your bottom dollar buster, Fat Mama was looking good.
Fat Mama wore these sexy little pumps, not too high, so she wouldn't topple, Fat Mama never did fall,
But she sure did wobble.

Fat Mama liked the latest fads, and wanted to look her best,
Fat Mama stuffed that fat in some jeans, and said
        "To Honolulu with the rest".-

Fat Mama went a strolling, a flapping and a flopping,
Fat mama went a rolling-
Down the stairs she went a c-r-a-s-h-i-n-g
Down the streets she went a flashing,
Fat Mama BeepFat
Mama Bop—

Fat Mama sweep, Fat Mama sway, Ain't nobody fool enough to get in the way of Fat Mama.
Fat Mama bounced, Fat Mama bowled,
Fat Mama just walked and did the belly roll.
Fat Mama wopped, Fat Mama rocked, Fat Mama rambled.

LABERTHA MCCORNMICK

Fat Mama's move was more like a soulful scramble.
Fat Mama popped, Fat Mama prowled, Fat Mama pondered.
Fat Mama's stump was more like a silent thunder.
Fat Mama glides, Fat Mama strides, Fat Mama pranced.
Fat Mama's walk was more like a soulful dance.
Fat Mama flings, Fat Mama flows,
Fat Mama's on The Fat Natural—

    Go! Fat Mama, That's so, Fat Mama!
Ain't worried' bout a thing-
_____

Fat Mama's on the FAT NATURAL SWING!

Labertha D. MCCormick°1987

Katherine Scott Florent

Shimmering, shining silver haze around her solely holy head
Illuminating the awesomeness of age
Sanctified sister, soldier sister, feisty sister, still sizzling
Mixing wisdom with wit
Showing courage and grit
Spirit-filled, strong-willed
With vigor and zap, gusto and snap
Casting whole-hearted humor
Always lifting the low
And still drawing eyes, turning heads, cracking necks,
And catching winks and grins
From courteous and gentle senior men.

Ngozi McCormick

BLACK STAR

Hooray!-ray,! Hooray! My B-R-O-T-H-E-R.
"You are making it to the top . . .
Got everybody cheering . . .
As you walk across the stage."
To get your Reee-ward.
~~~~~~~~~~~

You fine Black African American Negro . . .
You charmin' chunk'a chocolate hero
You sweet and sexy thang
You sportsman, you actor, you singer,
You rapper, you're a star.
"They going to
Wanna to see you some mo . . ."
Next time to get another even Bigger Ree-ward.
But watch out
My B-r-o-t-h-e-r

"Watch out."

Cause it's not until White America sees you in the raw entangled with some some white woman,
that they'll be satisfied.
    You heard me—Don't fall for it
        Don't belittle yourself with anybody.

Don't be sucked into the pitfalls by a downplay on decency.
And don't be among the common cut-throats.
What we need to see is you teaching somebody; teaching them how to read, or fill out an application with you being the employer . . .

LABERTHA McCORNMICK

*We need to see you out here on the Big Screen playing
a part, like Charleston Heston as Moses—
when God parted for Him the Red Sea.*

*Something we can remember . . . The wondrous works of His almighty power.
So we can call on Him still to make a path for us to walk through furious and troublesome ocean tide,
"Waters of our lives"
"ya' heard me—"
"Think about it—"*

*Peace to you,
My Brother*
Labertha D. McCormick©2008

                    Be sanctified—be set apart

Before The End Of Time

Before the end of time
The Black man shall rise,
Can you hear me?
Can you fully understand?
Do you comprehend my message?
Am I making myself clear to you?

Before the end of time
The Black man shall be recognized as a
Sole contributing factor to America and
Beyond through his numerous inventions
And discoveries greatly contributing to its
Prominence as a nation
An attribute withheld of his genius as a people.

Before the end of time
The Black man shall set in councils great
Councils and hold positions that he has
Never held before (in USA)

Before the end of time, the Black man shall
Flourish the White House so abundantly that it will
No longer be known as the White House but the Black House
Before the end of time, the Black man shall
Come to the realization that he is his brother's keeper
Not to be forsaken, that he can't be elevated
Until his brother is elevated and that he, in order
To be cultivated must bear the burden of his brother
Before the end of time he shall witness
An outpouring of the spirit of deliverance
And there shall be a reawakening of self
And broken shall be his forces of oppression

Henceforth, the Black man shall reap the
Unpaid wages of slavery that his forefathers sowed
Before the end of time,
The Black man shall rise
Did you hear me?
Did you fully understand?
Did you comprehend my message?

Be among the risen. Did I make myself clear to you?
Before the end of time, all shall be given the
Knowledge of Jesus—do accept.
                              (1987)

Strive to keep peace in your home,
There is already a war going on outside.

The Time is Short

Oh, My dear friends, did it ever occur to you that the time is short?
You who wait and procrastinate to do the things that should be done today

You, who won't speak to your neighbor when even your neighbor's dog will wag his tail,
You who refuse to make peace with your brother when
knowing you are the "Grinch" who stole Christmas.
You who encourage sinfulness by supporting that which is not pleasing to God
-The Time is Short-

You who go around breaking hearts while playing the part of
      Casanova

You who ignore your neighbor, while knowing they are in need.

    The Time is short

You who offer no comfort in times of distraught.
You who are taking your own good time to visit Mama Sadie, when she is already 99 years old.
You, who are smothered by the useless material weight of the world and refuse to lighten your load by sharing.
You who have the will to kill if your Lexus is scratched.

You who take delight in the misfortune of others.
You who refuse to believe that "it's not all about you."
You who, refuse to heal the broken-hearted by a simple phone call~
You who block your own blessings by gripes and senseless complaints.
The time is short
You who, spitefully murder the character of your brother.
You who through you own arrogance, selfishness and conceit have <u>not</u> made the world a better place.

You, who thrive on the spirit of discontentment.
You, who through your abundance of blessings won't spread the goodness of GOD.
You, who will not let the Lord be the light of your life.
    THE TIME IS SHORT

If you only could know and see and feel "all of a sudden" that
The time is short
How it would break the "spell"
How you would go "instantly: to do the thing which you might never have another chance to do* (Phillip Brooks)

It's not what you know but what you sow

(c) 2008

Tevin Clark

GARBAGE MAN

Come on down through funk town; and swing and sway your garbage cans.
   The Garbage Man

Come on down through funk town ; you fine hunk of a man

The garbage Man is the helper of the land who gets little recognition; but if it wasn't for him us folk would choke of a funk-a fied addiction.

He was nicknamed Lame Brain, Doe-Doe, Dumb-Dumb, cause he glided through grade school and slid through high.
He was the number one choice of none.

They thought he wasn't gonna be nobody.
They thought he wasn't gonna be no count.
but
old grandpa used to say,
"Somehow boy, in life you will make your way . . ."
So, you got to be a garbage man, just raising and dumping those garbage cans, just shoveling through the funk of the land.

Can you keep on truckin' after sliding through slop.
Can you squinch maggots without gritting your teeth.
Can you with hold a frown with stink all around.
Can you trot, trot, trot and not get too hot, hot hot.

Can you meet the qualification to fill the job description of a garbage man.
With no phony pride to hide the feeling of fighting the funk.
Raise up his recognition for such an honorable position so come on down.
Ah—Hail to the Garbage Man, he's the Prince of Funk Land.
He's the King of the Garbage Cans,

Sho wish grandpa could see you now.
They thought you wasn't goanna be nobody.

Labertha McCornmick

They thought you wasn't gonna be no count.

Ya'll folk wanna give so much acclaim, to this man called the president.
But if it wasn't for your dear garbage man, he couldn't make his speech for the FUNK scent.
So, come on down through funk town you fine hunk of a man, come on down through funk town and swing and sway your garbage cans.

The garbage man never went to no spa to have the body of a body builder, never had no practice on being a He-man.
—but he was muscle bound, strong from his chin bone, like spokes around his neck, like pyramids from his collar bone, muscles, wrapped snuggly around his shoulder blades,

criss-crossing his back, hugging his rib cage, muscles, humping his arm bone, balled up in his fists tucked into his waist,

twining his thigh bulging his leg bone, wrapped around his ankles, stretched over his foot bone, tucked under his toes, muscles—and you looking, looking all around for Mr. America—umph!
All Hail to the Garbage Man, he's the Prince of Funk Land, he's the King of the Garbage Cans, Sho' wish grandpa could see you now.

The garbage man wears no white collar. No blue collar, no black collar, but no no collar, no sleeves.
Oh, anything will do, anything will do for the garbage man.
His stinch might petrify you ma, but spell-bind you women.
Hey, garbage man, you just raising and swinging those garbage cans,
you wear that sweat-drenched bandana like a crown, swinging those garbage cans all around, you prince, you king, you beast of the garbage cans,
I see you moving on down. Whoa! Eldorado, the garbage man is coming, can't come through, Subaru,
The garbage man is coming, with a roaring sound of a mighty bulldozer.
He's trotting, trotting through the Mighty 9,
He's moving, moving on down Stench Alley,
Coming cross Funk Aroma Row, he's humping, humping toward Stinky Boulevard,
He's leaping, leaping on down Pew Scent Parkway on round to Wrenched Smelling Avenue, jumping on down to Nasty Alley.

Hey, garbage man, didn't nobody have to show you how to raise and swing that can.
Hey, garbage man, didn't nobody have to show you how to board that truck With one hand, didn't nobody have to show you how to be a garbage man.

Oh, you street joggers, you mighty trash truck trotters, I never see you take a break—And tell me how can you smile.
Let's all give a grand salute to the garbage men across the nation, cause if it wasn't for them, us folk would die of funk—a fied inhalation.
SO, come on down through funk town you fine hunk of a man, come on down through funk ground and swing and sway your garbage cans.

Ah—Hail to the Garbage Man, He's the Prince of Funk Land, He's the King of the Garbage cans, Sho' wish grandpa could see you now.
LDM. 1988 ©

PEOPLE DON'T BE MEANING WHAT THEY SAY

People don't be meaning what they say
    Talking bout they like poetry
    Talking bout they like jazz
People just be sitting there fooling you
Trying to make you think they got class.

People don't be meaning what they say
People will say, "How do you do?"
    Others will say, "Fine how are you?"
Now you know:
    Those people be lying.
You know:
    Those people ain't doing fine.
People don't be meaning what the say.
    People don't be meaning what they do.
People that grab you and hug you will later be the same ones that beat and mug you.

People don't be meaning what they do.
Them same people that love and hold you will later act like they never knowed you.

People don't be meaning what they say,
People don't be meaning what they do.

People will say, "Glad to meet you", and in one way or another be trying to beat you.
People don't be meaning what they say,

You could be looking a mess and people will say you look your best.

I'm a people, so are you, now you know the things that people will do.
People don't be meaning what they say.

People sometimes don't be meaning what they say.
You will fool around and lose your life, if you get sold on people's advice.
Cause
       People don't be meaning what they say.

LDM © 1990

LABERTHA MCCORNMICK

NO MATTER WHAT THEY SAY

Who are They?

They are the ones who suppress me.
They are the ones who make small of my life.
They are the ones who don't value my living—breathing—being,
They are the ones who block the growth of my spirit, stifle the progress of my intellect.

They are the ones who show no mercy,
They are the ones who say there's no place for me,
They're the ones.
They're the ones.
I am gonna stand in this foreign land,
no matter what they say.
I'm gonna reach the peak and not be stifled by defeat,
no matter what they say.
I'm gonna reach my goal, one that nobody else can hold, no matter
What they say.

I am gonna spread God's word, until every ear has heard,
My purpose I shall serve, and reap the blessing I deserve,
no matter what they say.
I am gonna beat the odds, in believing in my God No matter,
no matter, no matter what they say.

Labertha McCormick ©1985

POETIC PLEAS

I really want to make you happy; cause I see that you are sad.
I'd like to exchange for you happiness, for all the things that's bad.
Sometimes poetic moods don't take away the solitude.
Sometimes poetic pleas just cannot reach to those it preached.
Sometimes poetic deeds don't intercede
Sometime poetic styles cannot supply your face a smile.

I am just a poet, whom sometimes is paid no attention. And I hope these
words I offer you, be surely worth the mention.
Can't take away from you misfortune
Can't take away your solitude.
But maybe a poetic message might take away that sad old blues.
I can't dance for you the dance you do.
Can't sing for you no song.
A poetic word is the best thing I do
Hoping happiness will come along
Just remember that for your misfortune will one day be history,
Not to be repeated within the time there is to be.
And all good things will come to you if you sow life's garment well;
And the words of your good fortune you'll live to tell.
I really want to make you happy.
Through poetic words, poetic thoughts, poetic pleas.

LaBertha D. McCormick ©1985

THE PROJECT

Why y'all wan' ta be so hard on folk living in the project?
I was born in and raised in the project.

Close your eyes and you can't tell if the air you breathe is coming out of the East; or coming out of the project.
Ain't nothing wrong with living in the project.

Pork chop and mustard greens-
Smell some good cooking in the kitchens in the East.
Pork chop and mustard greens-
Smell some good cooking in the kitchens in the project, too-"

They got bars in the windows in the East; and bars in the windows in the projects.
> Ain't nothing wrong with living in the projects.

The sky is blue in the East; and blue in the project.
The grass is green in the East; and green in the project.
They got brown brick houses in the East, and brown brick in the Projects.
Ain't nothing wrong with living in the project.

Them mices and roaches hidden out in the walls of the East; looks just like them mices and roaches running all round up in the project.

The project ain't nothing but a piece of the East.

The got arrows pointing to the West; they got arrows pointing to the East.

The same arrow that pointing to the East is pointing to the projects.

The folks in the East is trying to get away from the folks in the city ; The folks in the city is trying to get away from the folks in the projects.
Ain't nothing wrong with living in the project.

There are some "bad pads "-in the project.
You ever check 'em out—

All decked out with them furniture from La Horne and Levitans, nice, you know?
They be decorated with them lil 'Woolworth Do Ditty—What Nots.
Close and open your eyes And you don't know if you're stepping up in the East, or stepping up in the project.
Ain't nothing wrong with living in the projects.

You ever check out them dudes coming out the East?
Next to them dudes coming out the project; with them faded jeans and no name shoes.

Look like them dudes coming out the project ought to be coming out the East and them dudes coming out the East ought to be coming out the project.

You'll never know I came out he project 'cause I be clean with my Jordache Jeans and my name brand Thom McCans... $65.

Them some bad mothers.
    Ain't nothing wrong with living in the project.

The projects got the biggest dance floor in town.
Don't cha know?

Friday, Saturday, Sunday, Monday,
1, 2, 3, O'clock in the morning.

It be jamming from one corner to the other.
And that music be sounding some good coming out the project.
Ain't nothing wrong with living in the project.

One day I'mo be moved out this project and get me one of them bad mothers in the East.
I'm getting tired of this cut glass scuffing up my Thom McCann's.

But first, I got to get my gold tooth, chu no?
My diamond stud in my ear.

LABERTHA MCCORNMICK

Also two or three mo' gold chains round my neck, and get this curl together. I wants to be looking good for my Mama Jama.

Then, I'm a get me this bad ride.
So's I can burn some rubber riding down Desire Street.
Yeah, me and my Mama—Jama, gonna be looking some good riding down Desire Street.

Me And My Mama—Jama, goanna be looking some good."

SIGN,

____ "Diffy-Pop ____"

LDMc 1984

A youth relates to a particular era of time, to life in the Project when such activities spoken of are of normal expectations. He speaks of "The East" as a higher-class place to live because of the more affluent status that it once held.

MAMA'S LIL UGLY BABY

Two handsome people stroll down the aisle, take the vows, turn around, holding hands to go on a honeymoon, not knowing that they'd be the makers of an ugly baby.

While mama's lil ugly baby lay in the crib, waiting for his newborn ugliness to wear off, Mama sat trying to prepare a solution for the rest of her life, to deal with the genealogical catastrophic error of an ugly baby.

But she knew from one momentary glimpse that her baby would stay an ugly baby.

Mama's lil ugly baby looked like he'd been hit with an ugly stick in more ways than many.

Then mama suddenly decided that there was no need to worry,

She knew that in the world there must be another ugly baby, as ugly as he

So she brushed his nappy hair till it behaved and brushed his teeth til you could see the reflection of your eyeballs bounce from their pearly white gleam.

And after the big brush and little brush had curled up from their labor,

There was not too much else mama could do.

So mama washed him up, gave him a kiss and a big hug,

Mama's lil ugly baby just knew that he was loved.
Mama's lil ugly baby was treated so lovingly, he didn't even know that he was ugly.

Mama's lil ugly baby ran around happily, just like he wasn't even ugly.

But mama's lil ugly baby never lost no sleep over who would be chosen to play the part of Romeo

Neither did he wonder why he wasn't chosen the Most Handsome Dude of the Year.

Mama's lil ugly baby never played a playboy's part, mama's lil ugly baby, never, never broke nobody's heart.

Mama's lil ugly baby had been loved, so mama's lil ugly baby knew how to love.

And there was this pretty lady wanting mama's lil ugly baby, and there was this ugly lady wanting him too.

Mama's lil ugly baby happened to choose the ugly lady since he knew that she was never a first choice before.

So, two ugly people stroll down the aisle, take the vows, turn around holding hands, to go on a honeymoon, not knowing that they'd be the makers of a pretty baby

—Damani McCormick

☎ —Sister to Sister
Sister,
If you only knew, what that low down dirty heifer said about you—You'd roll over like Old Dog Rover.
Sister girl, You would turn countless cart-wheels, Jump over 10 telephone poles—
Do fifty flips backwards, Do multiple Tarzan swings from the world's tallest tree tops.
Leap over the Mighty Mississippi River.
Slap 10 open jaw alligators in the face...
Huff and puff and blow down the brick house...
Glide down the falls of Niagara.
Land on a rock—sit on a stump
And
While catching your breath, with your chin in you hands, you may then begin to realize How much like those Low—down dirty heifers
    You yourself really are...
If you only knew—

With loves truths,
Sister—to—sister

        Be careful always
        When you hear
        The transferred thoughts
        Of a listening ear

SMILE

LICKING MY TEARS
    FROM
        SIDE TO SIDE

I CRACKED—
        A Smile

2000

PEOPLE OF THE RAIN

Rain, the rain
Rain, the rain
We are a people, a people of the rain.

All nations have pain,
But we, black people are a people of the rain.
We are a people, a people of the rain.

The rain of confusion,
The rain of mistrust.
The rain of seclusion.
The rain of disgust.
We are a people, a people of the rain.

We are a people of the rain.
The rain of fakism.
The rain of tokenism.
The rain of racism.
The rain of capitalism.

The rain, the rain.
We are a people, a people of the rain.

We are a people, a people of the rain.
The rain of oppression.
The rain of degradation.

The rain of pain.
Rain, the rain.
We are a people, a people of the rain.

We are a people of the rain.
The rain of deception
The rain of rejection; with no exception.
We are a people, a people of the rain.

We are a people of the rain.
We are a people of the rain.
The rain of strain.
The rain of rain.

The rain of determination; to attain.
-that whichever we have a claim.
We are a people of the rain.

Rain, the rain, rain the rain.
We are a people; a people of the rain.
We are a people of the rain.

MY MANSION

Oh, my Lord, you've given me much-
But within my natural greed of being human; I surrender to my wants and ask for more.
Yet, to the impoverished, I am rich.
yet, to the rich, I don't even scratch the surface of their wealth.

In this modern government house of comfort and sufficiency, I am still plagued with a deficiency, I crave for more space...
Every room and corner is covered by furniture, beds, boxes or bags, as if it were ingeniously puzzled together.
Nobody builds houses for a family of fifteen. We can never say grace together.

The strip of kitchen only services a few at a time.
Others carry their plates throughout the house, dropping food and extending roach haven.
It's hard to serve everybody without bumping elbows and stepping on toes; we sleep in stacks as well as layers.
Kids can't spin around and play airplane without slapping someone in the face; which causes me to play referee.
To open stuffed drawers is one ordeal; to close them is another.
Everyone l o n g s for a corner of his own.

Oh, how I feel like breaking through these walls with hammers and mauls-
Like the "Women of Brewster Place."

I seem to capture a feeling of freedom and spaciousness when I ride and view the mystique beauty along the uptown Streets of Audubon, Nashville and St. Charles

The shaded mansions of Gentilly Boulevard, and to the East; to feast any eyes on those of Lake Bullard. Astounded by their beauty and vastness, with the silence of an unheard holler,
My spirit cries out-
"Why can't I have one of these places; so that we could occupy the rooms and fill up the spaces,"
With all practicalities, anyone could see that one of these mansions is just what we need."

Most of their rooms remain so unoccupied that ghosts have claimed their emptiness.
Through striving still for the Mansion of my dreams. Be it accomplished here or after, really doesn't matter... for I remember—
As it is written.
"In my Father's house there are many mansions, many mansions-"
And I do believe... there's One for me. (John 14:2)

Labertha D. McCormick © 1990

Can't NOBODY BOOGIE LIKE BLACK FOLK

Ya'll other folk are tops in ballet
The waltz, and square dance,
Oh but
When it comes down to the Boogie, ya'll other folk don't stand a Chance.
So, when you hear our music, don't get too excited, Just sit down and hold your seats,
So when we do our boogie; you won't have to feel slighted.

Can't nobody boogie like black folk.
Can't nobody bounce them bones;
Lap those legs,
Slap those feet,
Flap those wings,
Can't nobody move those things, like Black folk
Come time to boogie.
Can't nobody wail that tail,
Snap them nerves
Swerve them swerves,
Push the pounds,
Can't nobody get around, like Black folk
Come time to boogie.

Can't Nobody swoosh that caboose.
Can't Nobody shake a loose like black folk,
Come time to boogie.

Can't nobody roll them folds,
Twine that spine,
Jerk them joints,
Twitch that behind.

Can't nobody unwind, like black folk, Come time to boogie.
Can't nobody juke,
Ain't nobody ever shuck
Like black folk.
Come time to boogie.
Makes you wonder, makes you wonder-
How all them po' red-bean eatin' Black folk out the ghetto got so
Much of energy—

Makes you wonder, makes you wonder,
How them educated black folk suddenly! become so rhythmically—ignorant.
Makes you wonder if all those happy Granny Annies done skipped the beat
Of the young folk heart.
Makes you wonder, if all those happy-slapping feet ain't been struck by the boogie Holy Ghost.

Ain't no big thing in knowing how to boogie. Too many black folk know how—only one lil bad thing 'bout the boogie...
Can't nobody—boogie—like black folk.
    Boogie loose, Boogie long,
Boogie strong, boogie on—black folk.
~~~~~~~~~~

(c) 1989

"Know it alls" who tend to make you think they "Know it all"-
      Try to make you really believe that they do really
"know it all"-
      But
They don't have sense enough to believe that if they really did know it all, there would be no need for all the other billions of people in the world.

That Bone

*I, I—I—I—I—I Thought I told you not to give that dog that bone.
That bone, that bone the butcher's choice from the scrap box, lined with lean.*

*That bone, that bone whose savory
Taste seasoned the red beans, the white beans,
And
Tomorrow was supposed to season the butter beans.*

*I—told you not to give that dog that
Bone.
Sometimes—Sometimes—I do wish you'd treat me like that dog.*

(c) 1988

LABERTHA McCORNMICK

GOD BLESS THE DOG

And God, bless my children with your kindness,
Bless the prisoners with your meekness,
Bless the world with your sweetness,
Bless the water with your holiness.

And God, dear God, bless the Dog.

The dog, who's name is used to express the lowest form of
anything and anybody
The dog, whom you created as a companion to man; but whom man has
doomed from his coming to his going.

———————

The dog, who's thrown at by children, kicked on by grown-ups, run over by
cars, shooed at by the canes of old ladies,

The dog, who's underfed and poorly cared for by mean masters, forced
to Raid garbage cans, left out in the cold, held captive by chains, run
breathless by race betters.

God, dear God bless the dog, for who else after being kicked in the tail
for peeing on the rug would later scratch the door with a newspaper held
between his teeth,

Would try to comfort your fatigue by licking the cheese between the toes
of your dirty funky feet.

God, dear God, bless the dog.

May foolish things be swept away,
With the speed of turbulent winds,
And tossed into volcanic spins
Dissolved into the atmosphere
Of forgetfulness and time.

DIVINE Advice

You know you never liked me and couldn't stand my tail at that
You would have walked a whole mile out of your way,
just to keep from crossin' in my path.
YOU really never liked me.

If your eyes were two fiery darts,
You would have aimed right for my beatin' heart.
If your tongue was a gun, you would have shot me dead in my head.
And just for the sake of having fun, you would have knocked my teeth,
out one by one.
As a matter of fact with anything sharp you would have graped right
in my back you would have stabbed.

And if you could, without a doubt you'd form a fist at your wrist,
And would punch my lights out-
And if my name had any fame you would have slandered it to shame.
And if you were alone in my funeral place, you'd stand over my coffin
and spit dead in my face.
You never liked me.

And if you look were alone, where no one could see, you'd grab me by
the neck, and choke the life out of me.

So, when you hear about my passing, and I am dead and gone
Don't parade on to my funeral, keep your Black—ass home.
-And later to the contrary,
I died, as you read in the obituary.
So, you rushed on down to the church
And sat through my services for all it was worth.

Hurry! Hurry My Children

While standing around burial ground,
You cried one crocodile tear, Between a smirk and a frown.
You tripped and fell dead on your face,
While rushing to be the first to get a plate.
You nearly choked while chewing on a chicken bone, Cause all your food on your third plate was gone.
You nearly gagged while drinking all you could gulp-as you steady had them refill your cup. And you nearly peed on yourself while waiting in line and had to turn around and vomit in the toilet bowl, *just in time*

_____

Now you know you should have kept your BLACK AND UGLY ASS HOME

Then you slipped on some punch and fell on your butt.
And it took all the guests and their mamas just to pick you up.
And you hollered so loud and went into hysterics-
The best decision then was to call the paramedics
We found out later, from a call on the phone, that from that freaky accident you cracked your tail bone.
Now, you know you should have keep your BLACK AND UGLY ASS HOME.

Now you know we are all one of the many shades of Black.
And are all ugly to the bone, an ass is what you choose to be
You should have kept all three at home.
And if you think I'm being derogatory, every word I use is in Webster Dictionary.

Now I'm not being a critic as God made you
'cause that's between He and He alone.
And
—if you had asked Him for His divine advice—

I think-
He Himself would have said:

"KEEP YOUR BLACK AND UGLY ASS HOME."
Now, that I am asking all you readers:
"Do you think I am wrong?"
"Don't you think this sister would have been better off, had she kept her black and ugly ass home?"

LDM © 2009

Speak It

Speak life not death

Speak life—and live more abundantly
Speak peace—and live in harmony.
Speak—hope, and claim the victory.
Speak—trust and live by faith.

Speak healing—and be made whole, again.

Speak love—and live in discipline.
Speak love—and watch your power rise.
Let there be an outpouring of compassion among us, and let us walk in the light of obedience.

Let us share with generosity.
Our gifts

May the spirit of the Lord
Breathe the breath of life on You.

May he blow into your existence
Blessing, Redemption, and Deliverance.

To You, New Orleans:

LABERTHA McCORNMICK

SMILE

A noticeable crescent that forms an expression of facial pleasantry, . . .
It evolves from the soul, in spite of life's drudgery.

In realizing that people across the nation hunger
and thirst for a cup of clean water,
I refuse myself the pampering of paying
to have my nails done—donate—and wait on my new and glorified body.

Don't be mad with me...
I'm just the messenger.

To the wives— Wash the clothes, do the housework, shop
Cook, bear the children, nurse them, nurture them,
Be humble, submissive, thoughtful, tender, honest,
Loving and sweet

To the husbands—
Stop lying

Sister, tell the devil to go back to hell
And hide his ugly face.
Pull yourself together baby,
And walk by faith.

TRUST

Trust and confide
In the Lord
And know that he
Is holding you.

Ref. notation: Psalms Proverbs 3:5-6

LIVE

... so that when you die,
Your pet won't be
The only one who misses you.

-GRACE

Cultivate your life so that you can receive the grace of
God that He wants to give you.
"He who wins souls is wise."
—Proverbs 11:33

Satan I command you—in the name of the Lord—
To drop your weapons and flee—The Lord has given me authority
To walk all over thee

Black People

Wake up! You've been asleep much too long The others who are running ahead of you Have been awake since the crack of dawn

There cannot be great success without great commitment.

Talking tongues tell tails that time reveals.

Shame on You, America

Oh, America, you Black America
You White America: shame on you—

In indecency you've grabbed the devil by his tail and played
Ring—Around-the-Rosie
With him and all his adversaries.

Then you clutched his hand even tighter
And strolled down the aisle of the church
And like a virgin bride
Took the vows of vulgarity
Then bent over (to the 90th degree), dropped your drawers
And shook and wiggled your raw and natural behind
In front of the whole congregation,
As if to say, "Now take that!"
And we, the loyal-to-lasciviousness jackasses of America
That we have become, heckle and hee-haw in acceptance, As if to say,
"Show me some mo' baby!
Yeah, shake whatcha mama gave ya!"
While leaving the youth of today no remembrance of decency to reflect on.

Hey, White America
Have you lost your scruples?
Hey, Black America
Have you lost your cotton pickin' minds?

Shame on you, America
Pity... shame on you!

Must you wait until you've doomed yourself
To the pits of hell and be caught in God's wrath?
You'd better hurry and rectify these wrongs
You'd better hurry

Watch out...

The devil is a slick trickster
He'll have you hot, naked and nasty before you even know it
Learn and know his sinful innuendos
Your youth are yielding to you.
Put on the whole armor of God
And cut off Satan's head with your sword.

You'd better hurry...

THE SHIP

How can i not remember, though they told me to forget—the ship,
That carried my Mama's Mama's Mama's Mama.

How can i not remember, though they told me to forget—the whip—
That scarred the back of my Papa's Papa's Papa's Papa.

How can I not remember, though they told me to forget—the chains
That linked together my brother's brother's brother's brother.

How can I not remember, though they told me to forget the platform,
That bore the feet of my sister's sister's sister's sister.

How could I not remember, though they told me to forget the—tongue
That would have been taught to my young's young.
The dance, that stood me out among all others
The song, that bound together our spirits,
The drums, our universal heartfelt Language.
The customs, that signifies our identity.

How can I not remember, thought they told me to forget—the past.
But oh, they taught me to remember, to remember
From Washington to Reagan.
But with them I have no identity, With them I have no claim.
But THE SHIP bore no name,

NO Nina, NO Pinta, NO Santa Maria,
NO Mayflower—NO NAME—
BECAUSE
THE SHIP WAS NOT TO BE REMEMBERED.
The dirty and deplorable crowded, crowded stinking ship was not to be remembered.
Sometimes I feel like I'm the offspring of a queen, Sometimes I feel like I really want to know just really where I came from.-

LABERTHA MCCORNMICK

My royalty lies beneath African skies My royalty lies beyond the ship.
So, tell me about the chains, the platform, the tongue, the whip, the customs, the song, the drums, the ship.

Not that it will rectify the past and re-indoctrinate the present generation.
I just want to know.
No that it will dissipate my mind from the drudgery felt by my forefathers.
I just want to know.

Not that it will give me a four-hundred year ovation.
I just want to know.—

Not that it will sanctify my spirit and make me wear a grin 'till my life ends
I just want to know.—

Not that it will justify the cause of four hundred years of captivation.

Labertha MCCormick(c)1983—

I WOULD HAVE BEEN THE ONE

I would have been the one who'd jump off the ship during slave captivity.
I would have been the one who choked my master with his own whip
knowing it would lead to my own torturous death.
I would have been scheming, planning, conjuring plotting.
I would have been a freedom runner, rider, fighter, and finder.
I would not have lived to be an old slave.

I would have been that stubborn, belligerent, deliberately, incorrigible
slave who no one could trust.
I would have been the one who rode side by side with Nat Turner shoulder
to shoulder with Harriet Tubman.
I would have been Sojourner Truth's sidekick.
I would have been the one.
I would have been the One.

I would have been the one who'd choose death in objection to slavery
I would have been the one
I would have been the one.
But
There were those who didn't and because of them. I AM-

It was because of those who chose to stay in captivity until they were able to gain their freedom I Am! I Am _____

_____
(c) 1988

It was because of the over burdened pride-stripped Uncle Tom's and Aunt Jemina's—Courageous Endeavors and fervent Faith—
I AM!
I AM!
I AM... .
Because of the sacred blood of Jesus, WE ALL ARE

Poetic Bard, the Universal Thread © 1991

MCCormick, L. *© 1988
Awc©2007

THIS OLD SLAVE

Don't call the massa for this old slave
It's better for him that he's headed for the grave.

This old slave's not sick
This old slave is tired
He's gonna die. So hush...

This old slave's done planted the crop,
Done plowed the field
Done hauled the hay
Done worked all day
For not a red cent pay.
This old body is flat on his back where he needs to stay.

This old slave can get some rest that way.
This old slave is not sick,
He's tired. Let him die.
And hush . . .

This old slave done hauled the water,
Done stacked the hay
Done chopped the wood
Done done some good for the white man and his greed.
This old slave's had many a master
Done mastered disaster—In his time.
This old slave's done picked the cotton
Done shoveled the rail
Done worked and sweated
Done sweated and fretted.

This old slave's done carried the logs
Done been a real work hog—

LABERTHA MCCORNMICK

All his life.
This old slave's done lived six decades and a quarter.
Done slaved—much longer than he had' a oughta.

This old slave's not sick.
He's tired. He should' a been done died.

Why send for the massa to perk him up
And be sent back to the fields for just
A few days, and work him till he falls
Flat dead on his face?

As soon as dawning turns morning
They'll be on his case, with the same do or die
Work disgrace
To hell with the massa, I dare you call.
This old slave won't rise from this fall.
Let the last breath in his body be claimed
By the real massa from which he came
No longer shall this slave the massa rule.
No longer to be a slave massa's fool.

This old slave we need not save.
Before dawning turns morning,
He'll be in his grave,
And his soul will drift through the corn fields claiming,
Freedom forever, freedom forever.
So hush . . . and don't make no moans.

-LBMc1986.

———————

(c) 1978

HURRY! HURRY MY CHILDREN

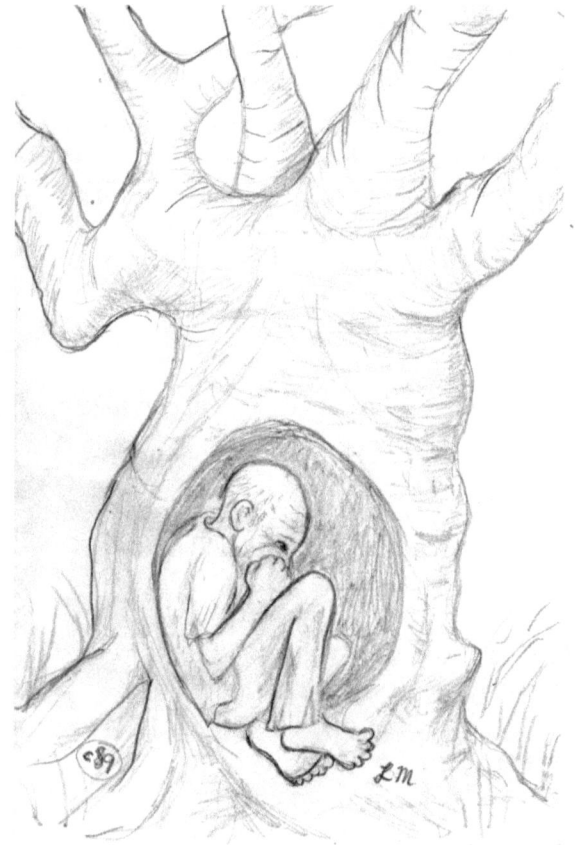

LMC9c)2011

DIRTY OLE WHITE MAN

Dirty ole white man,
When did you stray from skid row, into the big wide open park?
When did you lose you shoes?
You looked like you were a scarecrow in motion, too
Scary to be in a place of recreation,
So they chased you off to another location.

Dirty ole white man,
Truly you are your own nightmare
Your skin is so dirty and parched

LABERTHA MCCORNMICK

Makes it hard to tell that you really are
Just a Dirty ole white man.

Is this the way to treat a man who's astray?
For a dog they'd even called S.P.C.A.
Don't folk know they ought not to ignore you that way?
This is no way to treat you.
Don't they know you need tending to?

Dirty Ole white man,
You lay curled up against the tree trunk,
And though you're smelling like a skunk, you can take my hand and climb into my van.
Surely you are somebody's Grandpa.
Surely you be a brother or a Daddy.
Did you live such a wretched life to deserve this strife?
Were you always a Dirty Ole white man?

Did you used to be the one who'd chase lil' black kids
'cross the watermelon fields with your shot gun?
Did you ever take part in our suffering?
But what you used to be doesn't matter to me-
What you really need is a sanctimonious deed, from someone.

Dirty Ole white man,
Can you try to get into my clean van,
So I can take you where you'll get shelter and care?
'cause surely you'll die if we keep passing you by—
Dirty Ole white man,
Can you try to get into my van?
Can you try to get into my van?
And ride away
And ride away with me.

Six months later, the Dirty Ole White Man was seen on skid row

Labertha MC Cormick ©1988

Scars Of Sacrifice

Ann W. Cooper/akeia©2006

-Somebody's Body carries the scars of sacrifice—

Somebody's mother, father, sister, brother, aunt, uncle—mother-mother, grandmother,
Somebody's father—father, Grandfather-father . . .
—all whom in their yesterdays lifted you toward the Freedom Life.

Somebody's Human Body die in their Capture—Slaved-Oppression Struggle Times
to set you free.
Somebody's human body
-pick that cotton
—hull those heavy bales . . .
-cook those meals
-wash them floors . . .
-hung those clothes
—took the lash, got sold . . .

So, you could lay on silken sheets, with the finery of silver spoons, heirloom silver chandeliers, . . . All heirlooms of past days and claim the value of its workmanship.

So, you could live and be free-
—Today you can walk with a uplifted head and speak the proper King's English.

Somebody's, . . . within your bloodline tree
—carries the scars of Sacrifice.

Who was the the one in your bloodline kinsmen
That bowed & bent, Who?

-Wash them clothes, . . .
-Cook that meal,
-Hung those clothes . . .
So, you could step your feet in TODAY's
freedom Time.

Today, This day you can walk, talk,—Sit on the front seat of the Bus,
Take a meal inside a dining restaurant, get a degree in any college With
your head held high and your voice a beacon light. _____

In these Midnight Revelation Times, In Our Survival Millennium Flight . . .
-where our own Blood scars drip with open wounds,
—in Today's Battle of Life-Will you remember the souls of the ancestors-?
Will you raise your Voices in honor Homage?

Will you?

excerpt from Bridges of Our Lives(c)2006
      -LM

 —Oh, where would Mankind be had you not shed your lamb's blood . . .
      To set us free
       On
     The Hill of Calvary?

Calvary Echoes

Ann W. Cooper©2007

He was hung high! Stretched Wide!
    On the Hill of Gogathalia
He came to earth, A kingly Prince, son of The living Father God.
    Mary's child, for a little while in human—birth.

    He gave his life; A living sacrifice.
    He Hung on a wooden stake.
        Holy, Holy, Holy
            Without a spot
Lambs Blood pours from veins; His flesh—Man.
        —on Calvary

    Calvary!   *Calvary!*

    _____

    Calvary!   *Calvary!*

"There's nothing more powerful than a made up mind"
—Pastor Herbert H. Rowe

"Education without salvation is
damnation . . ."
—Rev. Sylvester Lyles

As insignificant as you may seem—you are significant

If your skin is Black
A
Double price has been paid, it is the price of Jesus Christ
And
It is, that of the slave.

AFRICAN WOMAN

I am an African Woman
If you don't mind
Within me African can be found
All the way from my African ground
And it's steaming, beaming-burning
Soulfully yearning.

I'm an African Woman
Gleaming with African rays,
And I'm boastfully broadcasting my heritage,
And submission to my recognition stays
I'm unchaining, reclaiming, revealing
My African ways

Oh, I'm an African Woman
Can't you hear my African cry?
That which they tried to steal from
My mama's mama
Is screaming and it just won't die-

Africa is in my dance and music,
Africa is in my song
Africa is in my everything
Deep down to my African bone,
And no matter how they tried to thin me

The African within me keeps
Keeps coming on strong
My heritage keeps coming on strong
And as God so intended
My s—h—a-t-t-e-r-e-d African soul be mended

And my heritage will keep

LABERTHA MCCORNMICK

Coming on strong

Oh, I'm an African woman
Though some may not claim me to be

My origin discovered gives me all the clarity.
Oh I'm an African woman
Though some may say I'm just a Black woman
Who is Black obsessed,
But what it is, What it really is-
Is that I'm an African woman, with African ways
Who is African Possessed
Who is African Possessed
And it's steaming, beaming—burning
Soulfully yearning . . . .

Labertha D. McCormick 1993

"In reclaiming all of my once-dismissed African heritage, I consider myself a self-acclaimed African woman, not allowing neither African nor American to refute me... Be in a hurry to know who you are while feeling good about being you."

If you live dangerously, . . .
you'll
make a wreck out of your life.

Black As I Am

Black as I am-
I'm not half as Black as I'm supposed to be
Black a I am-
I bear the scars of my past history-
Black as I am
I trace a trail of Black genuinity.
Black as I am
Black as I am
I'm not always judged by my integrity.
Black as I am
I cast my cares to the sea of iniquities
Black as I am
Yellow as you may be
Red as they come
White as you see
Black as I am
God sees the soul—Only the soul.
Culture is deep, so help it to strive,
But it takes the soul
To keep it alive
Black as I am
Color is free—and to nothing it amounts
Deep underneath is what really counts.
Black as I am
Black as I am,
Yellow as you may be
Red as they come.
White as you see.
Black as I am
God sees my soul
Only my soul.

To all Mankind-

As much as you can,
        L
         I
          V
           E
Without sin,
So,
Your sins won't—
      F
       I
        N
         D
You Out.

ANYWAY

People are unreasonable, illogical and self-centered,

LOVE THEM ANYWAY

If you do good, people will accuse you of selfish, ulterior motives,

DO GOOD ANYWAY

If you are successfuL

you win false friends and true enemies,

SUCCEED ANYWAY

The good you do will be forgotten tomorrow,

DO GOOD ANYWAY

Honesty and frankness make you vulnerable,

BE HONEST AND FRANK ANYWAY

What you spent years building may be

destroyed overnight,

BUILD ANYWAY

LABERTHA MCCORNMICK

People really need help
but may attack you if you help them,

HELP PEOPLE ANYWAY

Give the world the best you have
and you'll get kicked in the teeth,

GIVE THE WORLD THE BEST YOU'VE GOT ANYWAY.

From a sign on the wall of Shishu Bhavan, the children's home in Calcutta

Carry On

To Sr. Thea, Dolores, Carita, Nathan, Joseph and Bede:

For our cultural binding, you saw a need
Your dreams and efforts be not beseeched
But will be carried on,
Till our souls depart and drift,
From our Black African-rooted Bones

There is a strength that is within us
Embedded since our birth
A spiritual thirst that thrives
And doesn't have to be rehearsed

A spiritual quest that is in our being
Significant of our own
And it's planted, rooted, grounded
Deep down to our Black African Bones

There were those of us who were chosen
To pass on a legacy,
Of our true exuberant culture
And our true history

In servature of their ministry, of our culture, color and creed-
Of those who saw fit to carry on, were Thea, Nathan, Joseph,
Dolores, Carita, and Bede

Twenty years of empowerment to our people
Their dream will carry on
Through our heartfelt soul spirituality
In our cultural dance and song
The Black Catholic Institute: we'll carry on and let it live,
Through our Heart Beat Soul Spirituality,

That only God can give

In operating by faith,
Their yearning for culture and being spiritually led,
The Institute allowed our people to be soulfully and spiritually fed

There was a longingness to express—
Our gift for others to be blessed
They then saw it fitting to address
Our "Heart Beat Soul Spirituality"

Through their, music and their teaching,
Their singing and their preaching-
Their inspirational reaching
Of those wanting to belong

The Black Catholic Institute: we'll carry on
Till our souls depart and drift
From our Black African-rooted bones

To you, our cultural crusaders-
A spiritual light radiates
As your cultural drum speaks on
We'll see you again as we all reconnect
With our Black African-rooted Catholic Bones

Labertha Darensbourg McCormick

Tales Untold

There are tales untold
Of the brilliant, bright and bold
As legacies unfold
Truth of our history

Be it smite or smitten
Be it said or written
Truth be prevailed, not hidden
As ghosts let go the mystery

Measures high or measures low
Facts concealed be made let go
Surely you'll be in the know
About our true history

(c) 1974

An Old New Orleans House

I'll take you to this wondrous place
Where folk enjoy such cozy space
Where there's none of a kind
Like it to replace
An old New Orleans House

To wooden steps that lead you up
To shutter doors that swing open wide
Like open arms
Welcoming guests as if to say, "Come on inside"

Enthroned above these shutter doors are hand carved
Brackets that add décor
So magnificently shaped and
Skillfully done—as if God held the artist's hand—
And carved them one by one

An Old New Orleans House
Once your feet have carried you inside

You've graced the presence of New Orleans pride
You'll see wooden floors, beautifully carved mantle pieces,
Wooden trimmings and old fire places

As you enter into every room
You'll fill a quaint and lofty mysterious gloom

And as you gaze upon these walls
You'll see windows tall and ceilings high
For air to host

Oh, of the things I love the most
Is the presence of the friendly ghosts

Who lurk within these ancient homes-

To let you know
You are not alone
An Old New Orleans House

Now and then, there is a chance
Your eyes may bat and catch a glance

Within the space of the antiquated house
The presence of a cute little mouse
As if to say, I live here too within these walls and floors
And there's nothing more
That I adore than this Old New Orleans House

To add to this New Orleans flavor,
Is the presence of some nosey neighbors
Who stretch their necks and get on the phone-
Making sure that there is nothing fishy going on

These straight-through rooms led
One after the other,
Make sure the family stays close knit together.

An Old New Orleans House
Now
A modern house—Ahh—which would you rather?

A reading from the book of Sirach

A faithful friend is beyond comparison

A kind mouth multiplies friends, and gracious lips prompt friendly greetings. Let your acquaintances be many, but one in a thousand your confidant. When you gain a friend, first test him and be not too ready to trust him. For one sort of friend is a friend when it suits him, but he will not be with you in time of distress. Another is a friend who becomes an enemy, and tells of the quarrel to your shame. Another is a friend, a boon companion, who will not be with you when sorrow comes. When things go well, he is your other self, and lords it over your servants; But if you are brought low, he turns against you and avoids meeting you. Keep away from your enemies; be on your guard with your friends. A faithful friend is a sturdy shelter; he who finds one finds a treasure. A faithful friend is beyond price, no sum can balance his worth. A faithful friend is a life-saving remedy, such as he who fears God finds; for he who fears God behaves accordingly, and his friend will be like himself.
Become a faithful friend—Hurry

Labertha McCormick-2003

So Mo Hair Baby

Now gimme some mo hair baby, So mo hair
Let it reach past my shoulders
No—my back
Na-a-a-ah that still ain't enough
Let it hit my butt
Booty braids, bay-bee
Yeah booty braids

So mo hair baby
So mo hair

A-u-u-u-u-ah
Just get it on—get it on, get it on
Make it long, make it long

Now clip it on, snap it on, bip it on, bap it on
Dip it on dap it on, plait it on, wrap it on, tape it on
Tap it on

Just make it long
Just make it long

Make it long-so mo hair baby,
So mo hair

Na-a-ah sew it on, blow it on, screw it on,
Glue it on, fuse it on, do it on

So mo hair baby, some mo hair
Make it long, make it long
So that when I turn my face
It'll wrap round my waist

Make it long so when I bow my head,
It'll wrap round my legs
So mo hair baby
So mo hair

Now let it be red, red, red hot fire engine red,
No, make it orange, orange, blazing sun orange
Like the blazing sun
No make it blonde, blonde, blonde
Cause blondes have mo fun, ya know

Make it white, white, white
Cause that'll make it right

Just get it on, get it on, get it on
Make it long, make it long

Some mo hair baby
Some mo hair

Fa sho!
If we extended our brains as much as we extended our hair—we could wipe out a whole lot of ignorance.

I'm Not Really Crazy

Ridiculous, yet conspicuous. Meticulous, serious and delirious
But I'm not really crazy.
Studious, stupendous, wondrous and expundrous
But I'm not really crazy. *(a little more dramatic)*
Marvelous, prodigious, unusual and confusual
Despicable, unpredictable,
But I'm not really crazy *(higher pitch, more dramatic)*
exceptional and rejectional
Sensible, incomprehensible, unreasonable and unrelatable
Illucidious, stupidious, foolishuous, judicious
Fashionable, un-impassable, fantastic, bombastic
But I'm not really crazy *(drawn out, higher pitch, almost like opera)*
Well…maybe just a little bit

Be in a "Hurry" to embrace your beautiful mind!

I Got There

You thought that I was not worthy
'Cause we weren't from the same descent
You thought that I would never fly high
But the angels scooped me up and went
To heaven anyhow
I worked until I could no longer
I fell between the plow
My body could take no more
So my spirit went through heaven's door
And though you tried to keep me down
Yes, I got to heaven anyhow
I rose above your whip
And I rose beyond the cloud
Although you tried to keep me down
I got to heaven anyhow
Heaven is where freedom reigns
Where there is no whip and there are no chains
There are no commands, no words, nor wants
From ruling hands, no do's no don'ts
Nor bends nor bows
Where folks such as you are not allowed
While slaving for your need and greed
I rose between the whip and plow
Carried by the angels' shroud,
BEAT, WEAK AND MEASLEY ME, ROSE TO THE EPITOMY.
To a place where you wouldn't think I'd be
And got to heaven anyhow.

My People

*My people, my people
Throw down your weapons
Throw down you knives
You're destroying your future
You're destroying your good lives.*

*My people, My people
Love one another
Don't stain your hands
With the blood of your brother*

*My people, My People
Stamp out drug use
Don't be the victims
Of your own self-abuse
And
Woe to the aftermath if you don't take caution
And God takes his wrath.*

My People

LDMC 1992

When The Trumpet Sounds

When the Trumpet Sounds
Will your feet be placed on solid ground
Or will you be wrenched, wicked vain and low down,
when the trumpet sounds?

Will you be mending and pacifying the emotions of men
Or will you be whaling and waddling and swimming in sin
        When the trumpet sounds?
Will you be bellowing and cussing with a dirty mouth,
And a great contributor to the Dirty South

Will you be running rampant with the sinful majority.
Or will you be walking in holiness with the holy minority.
        When the trumpet sounds
        When the trumpet sounds.

Will you be lying with an unlawful lover,
If this be so, don't run for cover-
        When the trumpet sounds
        When the trumpet sounds . . .

Will you be following the 10 Commandments of Moses, or waddling
and rollin' in wine, women and roses . . .
When the trumpet sounds?

Will you be helping to guide the wayward lives,
> Or will you be part of the problem of guns and
knives?
Will you be feeding the hungry and clothing the
needy
Or grabbing all you can, being selfish and greedy.
> When the trumpet sounds?

Will you be bopping, rockin' or booty-poppin'
Or sneaking, creeping or bar-room hoppin'
When the trumpet sounds?
When the trumpet sounds, will you be living a good Christian life, by trying to win more souls for Christ?
When the trumpet sounds Will you be heaven sent or hell bound.
When the trumpet sounds?

LBDMC1990

I came

I shall dwell within the hearts of men
If they decided to let me in

I'm shown within the works and deeds of those whose lives they intercede.
I'm shown within the caring touch of those who need to be loved much
I've shown within the thirst of men, that can be quenched by loving trends.
I've shown within the homeless folk, who need you to share your many coats.
I'm shown within the many hearts of men who comfort the lonesome and become their friend.
I'm shown within the sharing of shoes—to those who have no pairs to chose.

So, when you hear me knock
Do let me in
I came before—and I'll come again-

Tomorrow

I woke up on he right side of the bed, but with a crow's foot creasing the corner of my left eye,
And somehow I couldn't spring up right away, and somehow I had that *'just woke'* look all day.
That's tomorrow coming, bringing all it's unwanted guests—from sags to bags, lines to wrinkles, firm flesh to fat flab and wondering where's my diminishing hair . . . just breaking down this *'Brick House'*
That's *old saying*—" Hi! That's *old telling young*—"Bye Bye."

"But ooooh, tomorrow ain't got no stuff for me.
I've formulated my own Ambiolaynadinatraesoterfiancema." I mix it by the pound, use it by the ounce, everyday, all over. I know tomorrow's coming-.
Mother nature ain't gonna mess with this. I don't play that getting old stuff—Ugh—Ugh . . .

Now let me tell you, that fat wanted to come live with me, had started shacking—up round my waist and clinging to my behind but I started squeezing and whipping that fat in advance and that fat couldn't stand a chance—sho' as I tell ya'
Sho' as I tell ya', but tomorrow ain't got no stuff for me. I'm going to hold on to my youth . . ."

"You see, while you be gossiping, trying to find out who's messing over who, and who done got messed over, I get into my secrets . . . While you be stretching your neck, trying to watch for the best-dressed broad of the block, I get into my secrets. While you be twiddling your fingers, wonder whatever happened to your good thing, I get into my secrets. While you be 'soap—opera'in watching white folks getting richer, while you sit there getting poorer,

I get into my secrets. while you be doing your thing, I get into my secrets.

I be natural-born working on rejuvenation, baby. I've got father time so confused that when I pass by the clock, the hands go—'counter-clockwise'—all because of my secrets.
Watch out Lena Horne.
And as long as money is green and seasons are changeable, I'll have hair to spare . . . that's rearrange able.

I've just got to tell you this. I even put together my own home made, age-blocking, time—stopping
Vitamin pills, triple and quadruple on every known 'you name it' . . . two inches long.
You want to know how I get it down . . . baby . . . I get it down.
Is it dangerous? Why sure, the thing might kill me. I ain't no scientist . . .
But if I die young, it will be from trying to keep from getting old. Ya' better back of mother nature.
"No, tomorrow ain't got no stuff for me, I 've got my Ambiolaynadinaraesoerfiancema, . . .
I mix it by the pound, use it by the ounce, everyday, all over . . . I'm going to hold on to my youth."

"Tomorrow needn't be told yesterday's truth."
Labertha D. McCormick 1988
Hurry, hurry my children—conquer tomorrow by preparing for today your heart, soul and mind... not your fat, flesh and flab.

(c) 2011

SILENCE

Day, don't break
Clock, don't tock—T.V. Don't talk
Refrigerator, don't sound your motor.
I want to listen to silence.

Roaches, don't roam
Mice, don't munch
Dust, don't settle on the furniture.

Wind, don't blow your cool
House, don't take this time to settle
Doors, don't squeak
Faucet, don't leak
Music, don't sound
Birds, don't tweet
Phones, don't ring
People, don't make yourself known to me

I want to listen to silence

Now, silence, I avail myself to you
And now that the way is clear,
silence, sweet silence
I can now hear the voice of my Lord.

Silence, sweet silence
He has so much to tell me.

Be in a Hurry to seek silence.

(c) 2002

THIS OLD BODY'S GONNA DIE

Send away the doctor,
Wipe away the tears,
Don't make uh no moan,
Over these old bones.
This old body's not sick,
This old body's tired.
I'm gonna die—so, hush-sh-sh-sh.

This old body's done shoveled the rail,
Done worked and sweated,
Done fished in the waters;
Done fathered more younguns the I had da' oughta.

This old body's done been through the wringer,
Done been a humdinger; In my time.

This old body's done gulped some wine
Done wined and dined.
Done dined and danced.
Done used all chance.

This old body's done wailed with women.
Done fought with men.
Done done some sin.
This body's coming in.

This old body's not sick,
This old body's tired.
I'm gonna die, so, hush-sh-sh-sh-!
This old body's done gave and got,
This old body's done a lot

Done laughed and loved.
Done lied and cried.
This old body shoulda been done died.

This old body's done lived six decades and a quarter.
Done lived much longer than it had a oughta

SO, Hush! Sh—sh—sh!

This old body's done walked and crawled.
This old body's been loved by you all This old body's done had a call.

Old body's not sick,
This old body's tired.
I'm gonna die.
So, hush—sh—sh—sh
And don't make uh no moan.

Endowment

      My Lord, come close to me, warm me with your sun
Radiate me with your light

Capture me with your goodness
      Endow me with your grace
      Touch me with your
           supremacy

My Lord, ground me with your
      steadfastness
Intertwine me with your
         love.

Surround me with your sanctification

Purge me with your cleansing powers
Laden me with your knowledge
Baptize me with your Holy Spirit
Indwell yourself in me . . .

My Lord, My Lord I am your vessel.

II Timothy 2:21

Let Me be a Poet

Of All the things I wanted to be
Serving you as a poet, really is the thing for me.
Just How? I know it, I know it, I know it

The Lord Himself came down to me and ordained me as His poet.
_____
Though they X me off their teacher's list when it comes to my position
But the stand I take in Poetry.
Gives me better recognition
Let me be a poet
You may call me crazy,
Cause I don't fit in the professional realm
But if what I see is sanity
I'd rather stay the nut I am
Let me be a Poet.

So I can make words dance in a story
Let me be a poet,
So I can give my Lord the glory

If I am thirsty and hungry,
Just give me some bread & water
That's all it takes for me to be,
The poet that I oughta

Let me be a poet,
Cause a poet is what I am

LABERTHA McCORNMICK

If I should become naked,
And you find the need to put clothes on me
Just drape me in a sheet
And put me on the streets
And let me be a poet
Cause a poet is what I be
—a poet, a poet, a poet

If I should become blind and can no longer see,
Sign me up for the first class of Rapid Brail Literacy.

Let me be a poet
And if I should fall from my wheel chair
Don't step on me, please.

I'll be on the floor crawling on my knees to the poetry jamboree.
And when I become old and feeble
And mumble the words I say
Just what you'll hear within the mumblin'—will be some bad a _ _ poetry

Let me be a poet.

When I am on my dying bed,
And have one last breath to utter
Just listen clear with open ears,
It'll be poetry without stutter
Let me be a poet

COMFORT ZONE

LORD—pick me up for I am weary,
I need to be held be you-

Hold me firmly, for I am heavy laden with the burdens of life.
Be careful not to let me fall back into it pits.

Now draw me close to your bosom so that I can feel the security of your strength.
Soak up, for me these chills as you cover me with your cloak.
Lord make sure to cover my head; to shield it from life's turbulent winds
Sooth me with a comforting touch; as I cradle my self in your arms
Whilst thou bring me closer to you-
Rock me, gently rock me
Draw me nearer to your face so I can feel the warmth of your breath.
Now, dab away my tears with your garment as they fall from my face.
And, bring me closer to your bosom until I can hear the beating of your heart.

Hum for me that melodic sound
That satisfies my soul.
and hold me close—even closer
      Closer-
           Even closer—

Ah ah h h h h h

LABERTHA McCORNMICK

    Now rock me 'baba'
        Baba rock me
Ah ah h h h h
Thank you Jesus-
    Thank you Jesus.

Now that I am lifted high above this troublesome world
Lock me In your arms ~

And never
    N e V e R—
        let me go.

Lbdm2009

In the Swahili language, 'baba' means papa or daddy

Hurry, Hurry My Children! translations

For
All the People in the World

Swahili: *haraka, haraka watoto wngu!*

Afrikaans: *gou, haastig my kinders!*

French: La hâte, dépêcher mes enfants!
Spanish: ¡El apuro, apura a mis niños!
Arabic: عجل, عجل يا أطفال
Hebrew: בחיפזון, לחטוף את הילדים שלי
Greek: βιασύνη, βιάζεται παιδιά μου!
Chinese: 趕快, 加快我的小孩!
German: Eile, beeilen Sie sich meine Kinder!
Russian: Торопите, торопите моих детей!
Danish: Hastværk, skynd dig mine børn!
Dutch: Haast, haast u mijn kinderen!
Hungarian: IGYEKSZIK siet, gyermekeim!
Japanese: 大急ぎ、私の子供たちを急がせてください!
Polish: Że, że moje dzieci!
Portuguese: Pressa, apresse minhas crianças!
Thai: รีบรุดลุกๆของผม"
Malay: cepat, cepat anak-anakku!

My Name:
—*Labertha*—

"Faith Keeper" translations

my name

in

Swahili: mweka imani

Afrikaans: een wat trou bly

I WANT TO GO OUTSIDE

If I tried to finish all these chores,
I'd never see the light of outdoors.
I want to go outside.

This window pane frame locks in my freedom,
This window pane frame game is driving me insane
Confining wails and conditioned air give me no pleasure
My body wants to feast on the goodness of the out side.
My self wants to be swept by the thrust of the wind.
My feet want to feast on the comfort of the grass.
I want to go outside.

I want to *loose* this window pane frame game from existence, and go beyond those walls that trap my soul.
Outside is where I want to be,
Among the birds and amidst the trees.
I'm goin' to walk outside and let the screen door slam,
Slam, so the world can know outside is where I *am*.

Then head gon' tell body what to do and body gon' beckon to mind and mind gon' beckon to spine and concentrate on motion.
Thighs gon' beckon to knees and knees gon' bend so legs can be in action,

Feet gon' follow legs and toes gon' wiggle on feet, cause toes are happy to be tickled by the grass.
Grass gon' surrender to feet and lay

down underneath their soles, then feet gon' trample around imaginary roses.
And arms gon' wallow in the *wind,* helping to spend my body around.

Bee's gon' come from the hive and beckon to butterfly that I'm *outside*.
Butterfly gon' flutter its wings and try to imitate my motion. Birds gon' circle my head and try to imitate my song.

And the unseen stars is gon' give me a sparkle and the unseen moon is gon' shine me a simile.
And the radiating sun is gon'my electrify me with a gleam making me feel good that I'm alive
And will alert my cosmic consciousness, just because I'm outside.

And I'll shake my bones and expel the tensions that hovered in me which then will vanish in the wind swept air. All when I go outside.

In glory and praise, I will thrust my head back,
Consuming my sight with the sky
and with my arms stretched out I will
absorb the goodness and greatness
of my God.

Labertha McCormick ©1989

(c) 1985

Big Bubba Lil Bubba

Big Bubba stretched out on the sinking couch with his big nappy head reared back; jaws stuffed with French fries to the max as he bites, twists, and turns; a greasy Church's chicken leg, as a biscuit being held in one hand is also waiting to be jammed in the other corner of his jaws.

Big Bubba's big red eyes tirelessly roll under the bridge of his brow as his mouth belches bad beer breath, as funky socks-and-cheesy-toes smell add to the room's aroma.

Lil bubba, already a chunky butterball, is also watching TV while devouring his third piece of greasy Church's chicken and continuously sopping and slurping his sizzling sodas, one after the other, enough to damage his young kidneys for a life time.
Po lil bubba.

Big Bubba is being begged not to switch the channel now because lil bubba is anxious to see gang men blow somebody's head off After repeated viewing, he is totally desensitized. Homework was never ever thought of.
Po lil bubba.

Big Bubba grabs the remote with his cigarette-butt-burnt fingertips and steadily presses and punches the remote control for more "R-rated" contents full of foul language on TV to satisfy his entertainment thirst desires. Lil bubba's teacher already says "He sleeps all day in class."
Po lil bubba.

And you would be wondering why lil bubba would cuss, fight, and like to feel on girls' boobs and butts so much.
That's the reason why he's always getting put out of school.
Po lil bubba.

Mama was on the phone telling Aunt Dot how she can get more food stamps. All big sister Dedi do is stay on the phone all day and talk to her boyfriend. Sometimes she used to help lil bubba with his homework but lately she stays gone so much when she do come home, lil bubba be already sleep.

She'll be gone herself soon cause she was overheard telling her friend Sheila she was pregnant and was going to go shack up with her baby's daddy.
Po lil bubba

he really won't get no help now.

Big Bubba used to help lil bubba with his homework.
But, after the second grade, Big Bubba said that it got too hard for he, himself, to understand.
Po lil bubba.

By now, Mama done grabbed her purse and done gone about her business.

After hours of such trash entertainment, both Bubbas fall asleep by the tune of the TV. What a lullaby.
Po lil bubba.

Lord Have Mercy.

MAMA'S PLEA

Mama's heart be heavy over heartbreak
That Mary won't come home.
Papa's eyes be deepened over waiting up for Johnny who loves to roam.
Grandma's mind be in misery,
Wondering when is Anna ever gonna come in.
Auntie's arms be longing to hold the one she hasn't seen since God knows when.

Teacher's tongue be tired over telling
Tina the same thing over again
Preacher's breath be taken over telling the young
Folk not to give in.

So, Johnny, please come home tonight.
Mary, please obey.
Cause Daddy's legs be lagging over looking for
Donnie who lurks the streets.

Mama's head be hanging after holding it up til
Mary finally comes home.
Grandma's tears be dried while waiting for
Sara to ring the phone.

Guardian's spirits be broken over missing the child she raised from one.
Auntie's eyes be eager to see the one she reared as a son.
So, Sara, please be good for them.
Joey, please don't roam.

Cause—Mama's heart be heavy.
Papa's eyes be deepened.
Grandma's tears be dried.
Daddy's head be hanging.

Auntie's arms be longing
to hold the boy who won't
come home.
Preacher's breath be taken.
Uncle's legs be lagging.
Teacher's tongue be tired.
Grandpa's mind be in misery.

All eyes be eager to see the one they loved so well.
So, Johnny, please don't roam tonight
cause somebody wants you home.

The Darensbourgs, 1953

A Letter to My Children

My children, hear me well for I find it most necessary to leave you with a message of warning and instructions for your life's journey as you are faced with challenges, encounter hardships and deal with the issues assigned for that day.

Walk by the spirit of the Lord and you will know His spirit by studying the Bible. Study scriptures and keep them hidden in your heart, for it is through the Word that you will be properly guided. Be diligent. Love and give support to your siblings as I see that you have done thus far, and I am pleased with what I see. Never let envy or jealousy come between you. Let your love go beyond the spectrum of family. Be friendly, give reference to your elders, show generosity, love unconditionally and share significantly. Help support others dreams and aspirations. In elevating them, you elevate yourselves. As much as you can—be dependable, but at the same time—don't be nobody's fool.

Be reasonable and avoid those who can't be reasoned with, at the same time, be peaceful concerning gambling, don't make it a practice. Set limits or it can become a trap. Be sensible. Be conscious of your company. Whether you realize it or not, they can be of great influence. Don't smoke at all and don't drink, for the exception of a pinch of dinner wine now and then—and holy communion—of course. Ask God for wisdom and he'll give you more than you've got now.

Always beware of any appearances of evil. Avoid getting caught in the gambler's web—it's a chance you don't have to take. Many times you will be surrounded by evil. Be aware, be wise, know the difference and flee. Be cautious. Be courageous in your actions. Be firm about your commitments. Be absolute about your morals. Be vigilant about your obligations and as much as you can, be genuine within yourself and yes, promote holiness. Remember your ancestors and pass on their legacy.

Don't think that you can plant bad seeds and expect a good crop. Don't think that you can do wrong and get away with it either—you can't. All sins have its consequences. Remember, God sees everything. He is forgiving and good and he is also just and merciful. Know that he tenderly loves you—no matter what. But at the same time don't temp him to wrath. Don't make any major decisions without spiritual advice, prayer and meditation.

You can reward or punish yourself by the way you choose to live. By the way—you do reap what you sow. That's the law of the universe. Don't be critical of others, you'll demean yourself. Don't try the impossible to please everybody. Don't worry about your enemies. God has a way of making them your footstool and bringing them to repentance. Be forgiving, be patient and trust Him, for he has a mysterious way of working through the worst of circumstances and removing all hurt in His time.

Pray and ask for a God fearing mate and you stay within His will so that you can be worthy of receiving His blessings and protection. Accept life, remember, it is God's greatest gift to man.

Over look—if you can—my blunders as a parent. I am quite an imperfect parent and considered to be quite crazy too—at times. You were good practice targets. Thank you for being my children.

You were worth the pain. Also, remember that in spite of all the accomplishments you may make, the disappointments that you may face—nothing is more important than the salvation of your soul.

Be kind to animals. God loves his animals and their purpose is meaningful. Remember one teaspoon of olive oil and bee pollen everyday and other good health practices that I have taught you. Share what you have to help others. Take good care of your teeth. It is important to your whole body that you do.

Remember to be optimistic, be content, know that God will take care of you. Know too, that Jesus is the light of the world. Share the light as well as your testimonies. Seek the beauty of things—it is there.

Regardless of life's circumstance—learn to smile, chuckle have a good laugh and even let go a great bottom of the belly He—Haw— release now and then and learn to lighten your heart. Be sensible as much as your sense will allow you. Don't forget to thank God for His many blessings pray increasingly—stay ready for Christ's return—consider all of this thoroughly—keeping a merry heart—cause a merry heart doeth good—like a medicine. Practice this in a hurry.

Love,
Mama

P.S.
If I should depart from this earth before the rapture of the saints, I'll expect to see you all in the "New Jerusalem"

Remember the one who laughs lasts.

A Kitchen Woman

I'm a kitchen woman
Ask me where I've been, my answer would be none
other than:

K-I-T-C-H-E-N

I'm a Kitchen Woman
Just ask me what's my name it's
quotation mark "Mrs. Kitchen Woman"
quotation mark "Mrs. Kitchen Woman" is the name I claim.

I'm a Kitchen Woman and I'm doing kitchen time
Ain't got no time for no devilish doings, with
Kitchen always on my mind.

I'm a Kitchen Woman, and the only salary I earn,
is rows of fat wrapped round my waist and arms
laced with Kitchen burns.

I'm a Kitchen Woman, my kitchen work is sublime
find anyone to be my match and we'd be two of a
Kitchen kind.

I'm a Kitchen Woman, for 15 I must cook meals,
and you can bet your bottom dollar buster
I can natural born kitchen deal.

I'm a Kitchen Woman, kitchen's where I'm at my best
come on in and sit down a while and be my kitchen guest.

I'm a Kitchen Woman
and to all you folks out there wanting so much
special recognition,
If you couldn't eat, you wouldn't live
so I even top your position.

I'm a chicken choppin, fish frying, green cleaning, corn shuckin,
biscuit baking, muffin making, dumplin doin, tater peeling,
stew stirring, pot scrubbing kitchen woman

And while my food is in the oven baking, I sit down
awhile and rest my kitchen nerves, and do some
kitchen contemplating.

I'm a Kitchen Woman
No other floor is drier and cleaner, don't want
none of ya'll folk
to slip down and charge me of no kitchen
misdemeanor.

I'm a Kitchen Woman
and to all you gals messing round in the kitchen,
making all those kitchen blunders,
due to the fact, you're no Kitchen Woman,
It's no darn kitchen wonder,

I'm a Kitchen Woman,
and though Broadway lights may never shine my name,
If anything I ever gain, it's gonna be some kitchen fame.

I'm a Kitchen Woman and from the kitchen grease that pops.

I learned to do this back-jump-shuffle and it's
called the Kitchen Hop!

I'm a Kitchen Woman and through all my kitchen
notions, I done developed this here new kitchen walk
and it's called the Kitchen Motion.

LABERTHA MCCORNMICK

I'm a Kitchen, Kitchen, Woman
I'm a Kitchen, Kitchen, Woman

I'm a Kitchen Woman
I'm a Kitchen Woman

I'm a Kitchen, Kitchen, Woman
I'm a Kitchen, Kitchen, Woman

I'm a Kitchen, Woman
I'm a Kitchen Woman

Age

Creeping, crawling into the doors of your youth
Who am I?
I am A... G... E
Accept me, if you will
Accept me, if you will
I'll change your fast and sporadic pace
To one that's slow, cool, calm
Yet full of grace
And I am wise and full of advice
Ask me, Ask me
And from what I tell you
You won't have to think twice
And to all you old sassy gals
Wanting to cover your gray
Don't part your hair and show your scalp
Or I'll certainly tell your age
To you old flirty men out there
Trying to play that young girl-chasing game
Come time for action
I'll tell on your years, and make you shame
To you old dancing fools out there
Trying to do those young folk dance and clown
I'll cripple your legs and tangle your feet
And knock you down to the ground
I'll toss you around between silver and golden
One title of which you will be holding
I'll pick you up just to let you down
As I slowly tell your age.
For some I may come fast and for others I may come slow
But I'll be on everybody's time, until you go.
I am age, accept me if you will.

Courageous Men

Up rose a hero who will forever be in the hearts of those
who were blessed to live during his era and his profound legacy will live on.

Nelson Mandela was a most courageous fellow-but
Cou-ra-geous men don't die.

Graced with resilience they carry on the sword of righteousness
for all to see and exemplify

Cou-ra-geous men don't die,

They break the barrier of fear
And hold up high the royal banner
of honor for all to remember them
by

Mandela marched and carried the
torch against Apartheid and civil
oppression.

He showed holy boldness and
served his country with firmness
commitment and bravery.

Cou-ra-geous men don't die

He was an active forbearer
A soldier superior, demonstrating
his leadership sublime.

He walked in the march for civil rights
He marched and he carried the torch
An active forbearer, a father in leadership
Cou-ra-geous men don't die

They carry on a legacy of strength
For all to see and exemplify
They carry a staff of firmness and truth
And make clear the path for our oncoming youth
Courageous men have vigor and valor,
Steadfastness and faith
Endowed with God's mercy
Endowed with God's grace
I tell you, these men don't die, but make it well for you and I
To trod the journey of life
By abolishing injustice, endured suffering and strife.

And so the angels carried our courageous men
To a special place of
reservation
'Round heaven's bend

Cou-ra-geous men don't die

(Be in a hurry to live courageously)

Special recognition is given to Mr. Melvin Lazard Sr. who fought for civil rights, and was also a courageous man who deserves to be honored.

DESIDERATA

Go placidly amid the noise & haste & remember what peace there may be in silence. As far as possible without surrender be on good terms with all persons. Speak your truth quietly & clearly; and listen to others, even the dull & ignorant; they too have their story. Avoid loud & aggressive persons; they are vexations to the spirit. If you compare yourself with others, you may become vain & bitter; for always there will be greater & lesser persons than yourself. Enjoy your achievements as well as your plans. Keep interested in your own career, however humble; it is a real possession in the changing fortunes of time. Exercise caution in your business affairs; for the world is full of trickery. But let this not blind you to what virtue there is; many persons strive for high ideals; and everywhere life is full of heroism. Be yourself. Especially, do not feign affection. Neither be cynical about love; for in the face of all aridity & disenchantment it is perennial as the grass. Take kindly the counsel of the years, gracefully surrendering the things of youth. Nurture strength of spirit to shield you in sudden misfortune. But do not distress yourself with imaginings. Many fears are born of fatigue & loneliness. Beyond a wholesome discipline, be gentle with yourself. You are a child of the universe, no less than the trees & the stars; you have a right to be here. And whether or not it is clear to you, no doubt the universe is unfolding as it should. Therefore be at peace with God, whatever you conceive Him to be, and whatever your labors & aspirations, in the noisy confusion of life keep peace with your soul. With all its sham, drudgery & broken dreams, it is still a beautiful world. Be careful. Strive to be happy.

(Author Unknown)

Birth Blooming

Stepping forward I stretch forth my arms welcoming you as parents into our lives, thanking you for allowing me to share in the gift of creativity, linked with its opportunities unsurpassed.

Thank you for allowing me to exist and be partakers in the building and shaping of our nation. I appreciate being an heir of the greatness of our people, who through their sufferings we evolved as the manifestation of miracles performed.

Hey! Look at me, I am your peak performance as parents—a unique depiction of two people who allowed this sweet interruption to take place and surrender your lives to the sacrifice of parenthood.

Hey! Look at me, I am the birth blooming, the challenge accepted.
Ex-cep-tion-al!
I am exuberant in my style yet I remain daintily flamboyant, and though I appear as a daisy, I am a sunflower yet to come.

I am glory of my parent's eyes and the gleam of their existence.

Spec-ta-cu-lar I am.

My song, dance, and every step are in honor and admiration to the God who created me? As I pour out my soul, I make humble my spirit and
benevolent my character in servitude toward my parents, my nation, but most of all in servitude toward my Lord Jesus who has privileged me to inherit His kingdom, for I am the offspring of God-destined for Royalty.
Instill in me a spirit of courage and boldness-a reflection of your sovereign majesty. Instill in me faith-the kind of faith that does not question the
"Wisdom of God."
Keep me in thy favor Lord, for it is within your favor that my blessings flow.
Keep me holy-in heart, mind and body-for it is through holiness that I shall see God.

Victoriously, the sword of The Spirit will lead me. Courageously, I'll stand. Diligently, I will fulfill my divinely appointed purpose as a servant to mankind.

In purity I will preserve myself so through the merit of my effort I may be made worthy of acceptance and worthy to be received as a cherished
treasure. I surrender my soul as a child/disciple and submit my life to the teachings of Christ, for it is through following His word that I am made truly successful. And let esteem not be in myself, but in the waters of the word that feeds me.
Hey! Look at me, a maximum manifestation of God's majesty.

He Speaks

Out of the depths of the deep blue sea
Out from the waters that flow from the valley
Even from under the ground we stand
From our surrounding land
From within the trees
Their blowing leaves
From the crevices of darkness
The corner we creep,
My Lord Almighty—He speaks,
He speaks Though we tend not to hear him
Our wandering souls He seeks
By his sovereign ways of grace and mercy
He speaks, He speaks
He speaks through puffs of breaths
At the moment of our birth
At the moment of our death
At devastating times
Within the walls of confinement
Within the willing hearts of men
Within the faithful hearts who struggle
Within our struggle for survival
My Lord Almighty speaks
He speaks, He speaks
Though we tend not to hear Him
Our wandering hearts He seeks
Through His sovereign ways of grace and mercy
He speaks, He speaks, He speaks
Through the beauty of the clouds
Through the source of the light
Through the blades of grass
Through the diversity of the flowers
Through the solidarity of the rocks
Through the slopes of the hills and

LABERTHA MCCORNMICK

Through the peaks of the mountain tops
My Lord Almighty—He speaks,
He speaks Though we tend not to hear Him
Our wandering hearts He seeks
Through His sovereign ways of grace and mercy
He speaks, He speaks
Through His majestic powers Through
HIS divine healing
Through His joy unspeakable
Through His miraculous works
Through His wondrous way-making
He speaks, He speaks, He speaks
My Jesus, My Lord Almighty speaks

MY GENEALOGICAL HISTORY

I, Labertha, am named after my grandmother, Bertha Edwards. She was one of 11 children of whom all lived to be in their late 80's and mid 90's. Among the many stories that she would pass on to me, this was the most memorable one of her great grandmother. Her name was Lovie Ann Curry, who lived to be 113 years old. She told me about how she would walk around the neighborhood selling pencils, with my grandmother being her guide, since she began losing her sight at about 110. She had become a freed slave at approximately 57 years of age. She talked about slavery when asked but did not want to put malice into their hearts, only precaution. She spoke about her last days as being her best days. On her last day, she asked her final question, "What time is it?"

The early arising resonated with her, even after freedom. Through our constant search and interest, my sister, Sister Rita Darensbourg, SFS was able to find the original copy of "Granny Lovie Ann" at the library in Chicago, Illinois after being given the opportunity to travel there. She remembered that Grandma Bertha said, "The people came all the way from Chicago to get her story."

*-Chicago Tribune, stored on MicroFiche film

AGED NEGRESS DIES

Lovie Ann Curry Was 113 Years
    Old, According to
        Relatives.

Lovie Ann Curry, A colored woman, who lived see not only her children's children,—but their children's children—died at the residence of—Annie Travis, her great-great-granddaughter, 513 South Cortez street, at 2:40 Friday morning at the reputed age of 113.

—Until a few weeks before her death, doctors said she was in perfect health.

The Aged Negress, according to her relatives, was born in Richmond, Va., approximately in 1804. She was the property of planters in that section of the country until the war brought her liberty, when she came to New Orleans.

While a slave she married Benjamin Curry, who died almost a half century ago. Six children were born, all dying before their mother. She outlived ten grandchildren and five great-great-grandchildren.

Old Slave Woman Lives 113 Years

Lovie Ann Curry.

AGED NEGRESS DIES.

Lovie Ann Curry Was 113 Years Old, According to Relatives.

Lovie Ann Curry, colored, who lived to see not only her children's children, but their children's children as well, died at the residence of Annie Travis, her great-great-granddaughter, 813 South Cortez street, at 2:40 Friday morning at the reputed age of 113. Until a few weeks before her death she was in excellent health, failing eyesight being the only apparent indication of her age.

The aged negress, according to her relatives, was born in Richmond, Va., some time in 1804. She was the property of planters in that section of the country until the war brought her liberty, when she came to New Orleans.

While a slave she married Benjamin Curry, who died almost a half century ago. Six children were born, all dying before their mother. She outlived ten grandchildren and five great-great-grandchildren.

Four grandchildren, Ophelia Robinson, Annie, Joseph and Edward Travis, survive her. In addition, she leaves thirteen great-grandchildren and four great-great-grandchildren. Burial was in Hope Cemetery Saturday afternoon at 2 o'clock.

Courtesy: NOLA.com | The Times-Picayune, New Orleans, La

LABERTHA McCORNMICK

GED NEGRESS DIES

Lovie Ann Curry Was 113 Years Old, According to Relatives.

Lovie Ann Curry, A colored woman, who lived see not only her children's children,—but their children's children—died at the residence of—Annie Travis, her great-great-granddaughter, 513 South Cortez street, at 2:40 Friday morning at the reputed age of 113.

—Until a few weeks before her death, doctors said she was in perfect health.

The Aged Negress, according to her relatives, was born in Richmond, Va., approximately in 1804. She was the property of planters in that section of the country until the war brought her liberty, when she came to New Orleans.

While a slave she married Benjamin Curry, who died almost a half century ago. Six children were born, all dying before their mother. She outlived ten grandchildren and five great-great-grandchildren.

THE CHURCH OF GOD AND CHRIST, *Hutchins, Texas*

Pastor Luther Claude Dixon

1903-1975

My grandfather, Luther (Papa) Dixon, was one of eight children, who watched his father's body burn after being hung for a crime he did not commit. Witnesses said that his mother, Amanda Dixon, jumped on the horse and hurriedly galloped down the road in attempt to beg pardon for his life from the sheriff, whom she was seeking. She met him in her path as he beckoned for her to slow down. The sheriff's words were, "If you are trying to stop the hanging, it's already been done." Amanda became immediately grief-stricken and plunged head first from her horse to the ground. Papa Dixon said that his father was known to have been a man of abundant faith and constant prayer, demonstrating biblical teachings to his children. In spite of the tragedy they witnessed, one we know rose above the sin that was committed against his father.

One child, Pastor Luther Claude Dixon, was able to be the one who preached forgiveness from the pulpit, passing on a legacy of Christian teachings.

Papa Dixon would often say, 'The strong shall bear the infirmities of the weak' (Romans 15:1).

My Heart

I pointed my finger at you to
criticize, Then my heart said
no, and I saw through God's
eyes.

I raised my voice to slander
your name   My heart said
"No-you'll be put to shame."

I raised my hand to slap your face.
My heart said no-then I thought twice

I raised my foot to kick your butt,
My heart said no,
You'll do no such

I sped down the street to crush
your bones, My heart said No,
God will handle you alone.

I grabbed your neck and started to choke-
But my heart said no-
God's spirit spoke

For your
information, I'm
content
And free, and not
serving time For
harming nobody.

Nothing Lower

Nothing's lower than a
whoring whore
Who sets up bait
With pies and cakes, chops and steaks
Be it fried or baked
And steals from the wives
The weakened men's lives
With false charm and glamour
Swinging a hidden sex hammer
Busy with fury
Like the vicious sounds of a roaring roar
Are the tactics of a whoring whore
With moves of persuasion
She continuously flaunts
The motions of a lustful cunt
She wrecks and makes smitten
That which God has forsaken
And also forbidden
She has no regard for
destruction
She caused
To hell in a hand basket
she is sent if she doesn't
surrender and decides to repent
To those who relate and all
The more, there is **nothing lower**
Than a **whoring whore.**

Proverbs 5:1-23
Proverbs 2:14-16

Only A Child

By Ann Refuge

Please let me play and have fun
When I am just only one
Let me happy and care-free
For that's the way it ought to be

And remember if just for a little while
I'm only a child
And I'll be grown soon enough
Just let me be

And have some enjoyment at age one-two-three
Don't put pressure on me and make me grow up too fast
Let my childhood memories be happy ones
Fond memories when I look back at my past

For I'm only a child
At four, five, six and even seven and eight
Don't rush me to be grown too soon
For I'll look back and remember things that I hate

Let me play hop-scotch and patty-cake
Patty cake makes a man
Remember please
And consider my precious childhood
And let me stay as long as I can

Problem Solver

Remember if you are not a part of the solution
You are a part of the problem
And you can't be a part of the solution with
Closed eyes, a drifting mind and a slothful
And defeated spirit-
So be energized and
JUMP HIGH in a
hurry!

LABERTHA McCORNMICK

Shackles

Chains were removed from our hands as well as our feet
And yet these chains, these shackle chains, were never
released from some of our brains.

Hands and feet may be big and strong
But, it takes the mind to make them more on
Tell me brother where are you strong?

Does it stop at your hands and feet?
Shackles be that powerful force-that makes you
refuse to take the course-
Of progression-and makes the move,
When only a brain that's free could choose.

Shackles on brains, make you continue to lose—a battle
that could be defeated.
So, my people, I plead
Now that your hands and feet are free, take those shackles
Off your brains.

Shackles be in decisions you are afraid to make.
Shackles be not speaking out when you should.
Shackles be in not standing, standing up for what is good.
Shackles be in leaving our burden for others to bear.

With reason being lazy and cause you just don't care.
Shackles be in material wealth: as well as greed.
Shackles be that lil 3 inch cigarette as well as dope and weed.
Shackles be in gin and whiskey and all that booze.
Shackles be in the spirit of resistance that you refuse to use...

Shackles bow down to brass, silver and gold.
Shackles be on young folk brains as well as old.

Shackles be on white collar brains as well as blue.
Shackles be on liberal as well as conservative brains' too.
So my people, I plead, now that your hands and feet are free, take those shackles off your brains.

They Don't Care

Now, pay attention to what I tell you
Stop trying to figure people out
Some folk won't like you

Even if you got on your knees,
Chewed up God's green grass,
Spit out fresh white milk
And made the moo-cow sound for them to fetch
The bucket and fill up over and over again
For no reason

Some people just won't like you
Even if you just walked like you might be wearing clean underwear
And remember that the air you breathe
Does not depend on them so
Keep a look of pleasantry about your face

And go among the vipers if you must
Keep on your full armor

Be victorious!

Be separate, be sanctified

WARNING

My children, while finding your way…

Be careful in your movement and

take precaution in your decision

about which way to go.

Focus on your final destination,

being careful of stumbling blocks.

Slowly take precaution of their presence.

Move in a way that you will not trip

and fall while going around and across them.

Don't look back or you may be thrown off

course and trip. Then pick up your, pace,

increase your speed and…. soar!

God's eyes are watching you….

Wastin'

You are...
Jokin' and smokin'
Rantin' and ragin'
Kickin' and clickin'
Baitin' and hatin'
Scantin' and schemin'
Chasin' and cheatin'
Bammin' and bitchin'
Hustlin' and whoin'
Fussin' and cussin'
Stumpin' and bumpin'
Dabbin' and dopin'
Fittin' and fightin'
Hurtin' and twirkin'
Ramblin' and gamblin'
Stealin' and killin'
Bootin' and shootin'
Drinkin' and sinkin'
Thuggin' and muggin'
Pants saggin'
Feet draggin'
Speech slurrin'
Vision blurrin'
All these energies are focused in the wrong direction.
By the Way... you are lost!
By the Word... you are found!
Hurry! Get found!

Waters

Surprising waters Rising waters
Broke tiding waters
Swelling waters
Wailing waters
Sweeping waters
Creeping waters
Katrina waters-as in the days of Noah
Bold waters
Cold waters
High waters
Bye-bye waters
Ferocious waters
Atrocious waters
Mean waters
Green waters
Katrina waters-as in the days of Noah
People, a myriad of people
People,
Caught by surprising waters
As in the days of **NOAH**
NOAH
NOAH
As in the days of **NOW!**

We Still Stand (After Katrina)

And still we stand
In spite of what the waters bring
Still we stand

Cause God is our contractor
Jesus is the man
He holds us in the middle of
His almighty hands.

YES

He lifts us up and holds us high
For all the world to see
How, in spite of all the catastrophe,
We still stand

Your Big Bald Head

Come on over here honey
And let me help comfort your mind
Lay your bald head on my lap
so I can help your nerves to unwind.

Don't go standing in the mirror
Counting the last strands that are left to comb
If having a head full of hair didn't
Put no more money in your pockets
They might as well all be gone—and

To all those old fussy mouth gals chasing
Those ole curly headed guys, and
Just can't seem to be satisfied
Must I tell you why?
They don't know the comfort of your
Big Bald Head.
I don't have to get no sticky fingers
Pushing them through thick naps and dreads
I just open up my hands and
Let my fingers rotate the surface of
Your Big Bald Head.

Don't go moping round the house
Cause your hair is gone forever
Don't you know a bald head is supposed
to reflect one who is wise and clever?

Don't be feeling low because your head
Can't give no contribution
Men who can't pay a barber for a trim
Don't have your neat solution
Nor do they know the comfort

Labertha McCornmick

Of your big bald head.

I don't need no clock out here to
Give me no accurate time
The hour of the day be told to me
By how your head reflects the shine.

To me, your bald head sets the pace
Suggestive of majestic grace
And it's all the better to see your face
That is so dear to me.

To me, your big bald head is pleasing
Sophisticated and unbelievingly e-lec-tri-fy-ing
Just to touch
I love your Big Bald Head so much
No other broad could understand
Unless she had a bald head man.

So come on here and let's go dine
Your Big Bald Head is right on time
And better still it's mine all mine
Your Big Bald Head is fine.

Toupee away, you no longer have to
Smother your head with a cap that's
Used as a cover-
You magnificent bald headed lover
And let them mock until
They are dead
As I said—
They don't know the comfort of your
Big Bald Head.
Now go make some money, bey-bey

Why Retire?

Why retire because of time acquired?
And smother the flames of continued quest,
With a blanket of relaxation and laziness.
Breathing God's good air and benefitting no one.
The burning flame of fire
That once housed knowledge, wisdom, and desire.
Acquired through years of experience.
Finally embellished into excellence.
Could so readily be dispersed and consumed.
By our yearning oncoming youth.
You welcome death much sooner when you don't rewind the clock of time.
Gifts need not be buried by the drifting plague of surrender.
Don't let retire, put out your fire,
But burn with the energy of servitude.
Until time consumes the flames.
Die dignified, die occupied.

Intended mainly for devoted teachers.

Gender Benders

Be not the one with a hidden agenda
Be not the one who is a gender bender.

Though you may be the borrower
Or the lender,
Both actions fail,
If you're a gender bender.

Switchers, swayers, and unlawful layers
Criss-crossers, vestors, vissors and vendors
Be all apart of the gender benders.

This message is to help,
The help is to hinder
The practices of the gender benders.

Though the written Word
May be tough or tender
It tells you not
To be a gender bender

You must be straight
To enter the gates
Through the Word I relate,
I be not the offender
Just hopes to negate,
The practice of the gender benders.

1 Corinthians 6:9
Romans 1:26-29

-Don't be mad at me, I'm just the messenger!

In leaving a legacy of poems and poetry, I end this book with works done by four of my seven sons.

"Make Haste My Children!"

Learn to love each other,
learn how to get along with one another,
Be harmonious,
Learn how to work together,
Learn how to need one another,
Learn how to protect each other.

For one day a lion and his pride
Attacked a baby Buffalo
Because it was an easy target.
The herd of Buffalos united
And gave the pride of lions brutal blows
And deadly hard hits.

The baby was freed;
However, the baby was the target.
So "make haste my children".
Be on guard
Because the lions are out there hunting.

—Ngozi McCormick 2014
Spirit Warrior

Still I Smile

I've been stabbed in the back by people I trusted,
And stabbed in the chest by people holding grudges,
And when I was down I've been kicked in the stomach
But still... I smile.

I've been arrested for crimes I didn't commit,
I've fell so many times I lost count of it,
I'm a natural born sinner, no I'm not proud of it
But still... I smile.

I've been lied to, lied on, and even lied myself,
I picked myself up when I couldn't find some help,
I've eaten some food that I know was bad for my health
But still... I smile.

I've been stressed out, depressed, and had suicidal thoughts,
I have war wounds from every single battle I fought.
But nothing is more painful than having a broken heart
But still... I smile.

I've been talked about and laughed at in negative ways,
I've been criticized but I ignored what they had to say.
They threw dirt on my name but at the end of the day,
Still...I smile.

I've been hurt physically, mentally and even emotionally,
But I never let negative thoughts take control of me.
And even when Satan thinks he has a hold on me,
Still... I smile.

I've been insulted, let down and even rejected,
I was betrayed, left alone, and disrespected.
I've learned the hard way to expect the unexpected.

But still…I smile.

You can shoot me down or stab me up.
You can kick me around or jab me up.
You can knock me down, but I'll get back up and
Still…I'll smile.

In spite of all, I shall not let my smile be diminished by anger,
And I fear nothing but God so I laugh in the face of danger.
I'm not dead nor am I locked up in a chamber
So still…I smile.

To anyone that's trying to take this smile away,
You have a better chance at taking the light from day.
You are just wasting God's time like my mama would say
Because forever…I smile.

-Damani McCormick '14
Spirit Warrior

The Spirit of Joy

I keep the spirit of Joy,
Would you like to know why?
It's got to be cause of the creative source in the sky.
Any doubt in my mind with negativity asking why,
It's got to be Satan,
So I know it's a lie!
You have to look at the beauty within yourself,
It really helps,
Not just looking in the mirror saying I need help!
Cause when you feeling all sad,
That's when you really should rejoice,
Start singing in the mirror,
Recognize that beautiful voice.
You got a unique talent and once you use it,
GOD reveals His light,
Trust me!!!
I can prove it.

—Percy McCormick '14
Spirit Warrior

Quotes From Jeremiah Concerning LIFE

- Work on yourself from the inside out.
- When you constantly worry, you are showing God what you think of His ability.
- Money can't buy a true friend.
- Never give up when life gets tough, remember, it's just the drama segment of your movie.
- Everything "you" want to happen in your life won't happen; a sobering fact.
- Choose your own path in life— just be aware of your chosen territory and everything that comes with it.
- Learn to control harmful issues in your life, or those issues will control you.

―Jeremiah McCormick '14
Spirit Warrior

It took me years to write that which took you minutes to read. Thank you for having taken the time and may God's blessings be upon you.

The McCormicks—1992

The McCormicks—40th Anniversary 2012

To God be the Glory.

Whatever you must do, do it quickly.
-John 13:27

www.ingramcontent.com/pod-product-compliance
Lightning Source LLC
LaVergne TN
LVHW091538060526
838200LV00036B/663